MAKING BABIES

THE TEST TUBE AND CHRISTIAN ETHICS

Edited by Alan Nichols and Trevor Hogan

Foreword by the Hon. Justice M. D. Kirby

Acorn Press
Canberra 1984

Acorn Press Limited
P.O. Box 103
Canberra, A.C.T. 2902

Orders:
P.O. Box 361
Collins Street, Vic. 3000

Published by Acorn Press at the request of the
Anglican Social Responsibilities Commission

Cover: Ian Heyward

National Library of Australia
Cataloguing in Publication data

Making babies

Bibliography.
Includes index.
ISBN 0 908284 40 3

1. Fertilisation in vitro, Human—Moral and ethical aspects.
2. Human embryo—Transplantation—Moral and ethical
   aspects.
I. Nichols, Alan. II. Hogan, Trevor.

174'.2

Printed by Union Offset Co. Pty Ltd, Canberra

Contents

Notes on contributors

The Rt Rev. Oliver Heyward is Anglican Bishop of Bendigo and Chairman of the Anglican Church's Social Responsibilities Commission, a national group appointed by General Synod to advise the Church and comment on social responsibility questions.

William A. W. Walters, MBBS, PhD, FRCOG, FRACOG, is Associate Professor and Deputy Chairman, Department of Obstetrics and Gynaecology, Monash University, Melbourne, and Head of the Fetal Diagnostic Unit at Queen Victoria Medical Centre, Melbourne. In those capacities, he is a leading member of the Melbourne IVF team. He is also a practising churchman. He is on the Steering Committee of the Centre for Human Bioethics and is co-editor of the book *Test-tube babies: a guide to moral questions, present techniques and future possibilities.*

Dr John Henley, a Uniting Church minister, is a Lecturer in Christian Ethics and Dean of the Melbourne College of Divinity. He is a member of the Victorian Government Committee on In Vitro Fertilisation.

Dr John Morgan, Anglican priest and moral theologian, is Warden of St John's College, University of Brisbane, and a member of the Anglican Social Responsibilities Commission. He is a member of the Queensland Government Committee of Inquiry into IVF and AID.

The Rev. Michael Hill is rector of St Paul's Anglican Church, Seaforth, and formerly a Lecturer in Philosophy and Ethics at Moore Theological College, Sydney.

The Rev. John Fleming is rector of Plympton parish, Adelaide, a member of the Anglican Social Responsibilities Commission and co-author of *Life in a test-tube.*

F. (Rick) J. Brown, a union organiser in Melbourne who has trained in law, is a member of the Anglican Social Responsibilities Commission.

The Rev. Alan Nichols is Executive Director of the Mission of St James and St John, Victoria, and Secretary of the Anglican Social Responsibilities Commission.

The Rev. Roy Bradley is Warden of the Avalon Community, Lara, in Victoria, and was formerly Chaplain Supervisor at the Royal Perth Hospital and a Director of Anglican Health and Welfare Services in the Diocese of Perth.

Dr Ditta Bartels is a Post-doctoral Research Fellow in the Department of History and Philosophy of Science at the University of Wollongong, and a Research Affiliate in the School of Biological Sciences at the University of Sydney. She was a member of the World Council of Churches' Working Party which prepared the document *Manipulating life: ethical issues in genetic engineering.*

D. Gareth Jones is Professor of Anatomy, University of Otago Medical School, Dunedin, New Zealand, and was formerly an Associate Professor in Perth. The issues raised in his chapter are more fully developed in his forthcoming book *Brave new people: ethical issues at the commencement of life* to be published in 1984 by Inter-Varsity Press, U.K.

Trevor Hogan is Project Officer for the Anglican Diocese of Melbourne's Social Questions Committee.

Foreword

The Hon. Justice M. D. Kirby, CMG
Chairman of the Australian Law Reform
Commission

The institutional vacuum

At the end of September 1983 I attended a conference in London
on bioethics and law in relation to human conception in vitro. One of
the participants in this book (the Rev. John Fleming) took part. Many
of the other named dramatis personae mentioned in the book were
there. Dr R. G. Edwards and Mr P. C. Steptoe made their, by now,
well-rehearsed interventions. They were involved in the first successful IVF conception, which achieved the birth of Louise Brown in
1978. Leading the theologians were Professor G. R. Dunstan, who
outlined the Anglican tradition, and Mgr Michael Connelly, who
spoke from the Roman Catholic tradition. The latter urged attention
to the causes of infertility, particularly venereal disease, abortion and
IUDs. He seemed to contemplate, as morally acceptable, the simple
family-saving case of IVF, i.e. implantation of all embryos created by
husband and wife, bound together by marriage. But beyond such a
case, the 'synthetic' production of human life was not to be coun-
tenanced.

After the doctors, the theologians and the ethics professors came
the lawyers. That was when I had my turn. My message was simple.
It was to express a concern I have previously voiced in Australia and
which is recorded in these pages. Like the diamond, it had a number
of facets:

- In vitro fertilisation (IVF) is one only of the quandaries of biology presented to our society in our generation by advances of science and technology. As a society, we must be more prompt and better organised to respond to the social, ethical and legal problems of issues such as IVF.

- IVF has social and therefore legal implications. The most critical of these is reviewed in this book. Is human life, worthy of the law's protection, to be taken to commence from the first instance of conception, including in vitro? Or should the law only offer its protection from the acquisition of 'personhood' or some other identifiable characteristic? Father Fleming expressed himself in no doubt at the London conference. In this book he repeats his thesis that human life begins from the moment of conception and is sanctified at that instant by God. No other time suffices. Accordingly a number of the surrounding procedures of IVF (which involve the potential discard of excess fertilised human embryos) are morally unacceptable. By inference they should be legally unacceptable.

- Unless we can develop a framework of appropriate institutions to help society to respond to vexed questions such as these in a satisfactory and acceptable way, the questions will not disappear. They will simply have to be solved by the existing machinery we already have for confronting and answering hard problems. In churches this doubtless means theological debates and the publication of ethical literature. In universities, it includes the conduct of vexatious seminars. The law's answers (in default of anything more coherent) are provided by the judges. This is the common law technique which we have inherited in Australia from Britain. In the midst of busy work dockets, judges are increasingly being deflected from property claims, negligence actions, interpretation of wills and application of tax statutes to provide legal (and moral) guidance on bioethical questions.

- Because of my conviction that these answers, developed in such a way, may not be entirely adequate, will often be developed in haste and usually offered after imperfect assistance and without adequate consultation on the community's interests, it is my view that a better machinery for providing responses should be found, and found quickly. In default of anything better, it has seemed to me that the methodology of the Australian Law Reform Commission provided a useful model for consideration in Australia. The earlier work of that Commission on human tissue transplants[1] showed how a controversial and potentially divisive subject presented to society and its laws by biological science and technology could be handled to general satisfaction. The development of a regime of rules after careful consultation with experts and the general community led to proposed laws that have now been largely accepted throughout Australia.

- Finally, beyond institutions, there are principles. It is important that our responses to quandaries such as IVF should be more coherent than the stumbling efforts of ad hoc solutions offered, bandaid-like, to 'keep the lid on' this debate or that. Yet there is a risk that this is the way such quandaries will be approached unless we can develop a more coherent institutional response than we have done to date. Judges have neither the time, the inclination nor the training to develop their rules against the criteria of concepts of a fundamental character. Ad hoc committees may be tempted to resort to no more perfect guiding principles than the will of the majority in the community at present. Yet this principle has obvious defects. In Nazi Germany, the will of the majority probably supported the outrageous actions against minority races, socialists, homosexuals and anyone who did not fit the stereotype. If we are to develop our laws on problems such as IVF in a principled fashion, we must find people and develop institutions that will identify the principles.

Court cases

Let there be no doubt that, in default of anything better, the courts will continue to provide their answers. Scarcely a week goes by now but there lands on my desk the decision of a court in Australia, Canada, Britain, the United States and elsewhere revealing judges facing up to the hard issues of bioethics. Take these recent cases in which judges had to address the so-called 'right to life':

- The Kentucky Supreme Court in the United States in 1983 decided that a man charged with assaulting his estranged wife and killing her 28-week-old foetus cannot be charged with 'criminal homicide' under Kentucky's Penal Code. The homicide statute did not define 'person'. However, it was held by the court that the common law rule should be maintained, limiting criminal homicide to the killing of one who has been born alive. The State of Kentucky had sought a ruling from the court 'in the light of modern medical advances and legal rulings in other contexts' that today a viable foetus should be deemed a 'person' for the purposes of the Kentucky murder statute. Two judges dissented. The majority adhered to the old common law principle.[2]

• In Britain in 1983 a woman brought an action against the health authority running the hospital in which she had undergone a sterilisation operation. It was established that clips which should have been placed on her Fallopian tubes were incorrectly located. She fell pregnant. She suffered anxiety during the pregnancy for fear the drugs she had been taking against pain could have harmed the unborn child. A normal healthy boy was born. She claimed that her measure of damages should include the increased costs to the family finances that the unexpected pregnancy had caused. The court held that it was contrary to public policy and disruptive of family life and 'contrary to the sanctity of human life' that damages should be recoverable for the costs arising from 'the coming into the world of a healthy, normal child'. Accordingly her claim for the costs of the child's upbringing to the age of 16 and enlargement of the family home was held to be irrecoverable.[3]

Unless we can develop institutions that help the democratic arm of government to offer solutions to bioethical questions, it will continue to fall to the unelected judiciary (and to a lesser extent the unelected bureaucracy) to weigh the public policies involved and to provide the answers. The courtroom is a good venue for the resolution of factual disputes between parties, where the issues are narrowly focused. It is an imperfect venue for the resolution of large philosophical quandaries, based on ill-understood scientific and technological developments and restricted to the parties and their lawyers—with little or no help from philosophers, theologians and the community.

This book

This book is the latest contribution to a burgeoning literature in Australia about IVF. It is entirely fitting that Australia should contribute to the ethical debate. We are, after all, in the forefront of the technological advances.

Professor Walters is surely right to warn us that IVF is merely an early species of a developing genus. How will we respond to cloning? How will we react to the claim of parents to choose the sex of their child? What is our attitude to genetic screening, when it goes beyond tests for spina bifida or mental retardation? Surely we will not tolerate hybridisation. Yet if we reject any of these developments, upon what principle does our society call a halt to such developments of science? Is it simply revulsion or fear? Unless we do something in the law, scientists will be unregulated and unrestrained. Yet if the law intervenes, can we be sure that parliaments and judges will be sufficiently sensitive to changing community attitudes? And in any case, should community attitudes be the determining factor?

This last-mentioned issue is addressed most usefully in this book by Dr John Henley of the Uniting Church. He was a consultant in the Law Reform Commission's project on human tissue transplants. Rightly, he stresses that we live in a plural society and that some Protestants are offended by the seemingly authoritarian rulings of the Roman Catholic Church on bioethical questions. Yet if rationality rather than authority is to determine the reactions of the organised church to bioethical quandaries, whose rational opinion is to prevail in the event of the inevitable disputes? Dr Henley cautions us about the needs for modesty in moral judgments on bioethical questions. But if we are too modest, might not the caravan have moved on, whilst the world waits for decisions on yesterday's problems?

On the other hand, Dr John Morgan points to the problem of the churches' taking a premature stance. The shift of opinion concerning contraception is used to illustrate the answerability of the churches to the opinion of their communicants. Like Dr Henley, Dr Morgan warns us against absolutist principles in a rapidly developing field of science and technology.

The Rev. Michael Hill takes us into biblical studies for such guidance as these can offer on IVF. But what is to be the guiding principle? Is it the injunction to go forth and multiply? Or is the biblical instruction about the sanctity of life? In the clash between these two principles, we see the quandary posed by IVF.

Father Fleming, believing that human life begins at the moment of conception, expresses his concern about the apparent indifference of proponents of IVF to the fate of the potential lives sacrificed in its procedures. His chapter requires us to face squarely the question of the beginning of life. If it is not the instant of conception, what other time can be satisfactorily chosen? Yet even if it is the moment of conception, is that determinative of the debate? Some will say not. They will suggest that ethical and, more especially, legal respect will attach at a later point in the development of the human embryo. Yet Father Fleming drives home his theme. If it is not to be the moment of conception, what other moment will offer a coherent principle? His conclusion is that in solving infertility by IVF, we are creating new and different problems.

Mr Rick Brown, a lawyer, reflects on the role of the law in this debate. Is it to respond to majority community opinion? Or is it to mould community attitudes? If we believe the opinion polls, the community's response to IVF is generally sympathetic, even among practising churchgoers in Australia.[4] Yet the nagging question remains whether that opinion has itself been manipulated by a media campaign of smiling babies and grateful parents. Is it an opinion worth respect if it is formed in ignorance of or indifference to the long-term consequences of disturbing what Father Fleming calls 'the sexual roulette' which has been followed for millennia into this generation?

The Rev. Alan Nichols looks at the problem from the point of view of the rights of the IVF child to know his origins. But it is not an unsympathetic examination. For example, he points out that the use of artificial insemination, the precursor to IVF, has helped those infertile couples who have used the technique to stay together and to avoid the ever-widening doors of the divorce courts.

The Rev. Roy Bradley looks at the problem from a compassionate point of view of pastoral care. Churches should not only preach authoritative theology. They should be involved at the clinical level in the very personal, intimate and stressful crisis of infertility. Dr Ditta Bartels, like Professor Walters, calls for a national approach in Australia to the response to the IVF questions. But given our Constitution which reposes most health care matters in the States, how can such a national response be developed in Australia?

Professor Gareth Jones, addressing the issue of foetal experiments, brings us back to the 'fundamental issue'. There is no escaping it. Is the in vitro embryo nothing more than 'experimental matter'? Or is it an incipient human life deserving of respect by ethics and protection by the law? This concluding chapter brings us full circle. Who will provide Australia, indeed who will provide mankind, with the thoughtful, reasoned and persuasive answers to the questions that are posed in this book?

Church and state

In a recent debate in the House of Lords, their Lordships were addressing suggested reforms of the English divorce law. Opposition was voiced to the government's proposal to reduce from three years to one year the minimum duration of a marriage before a divorce can be sought.

Some bishops of the Church of England opposed the amendments. They protested that one year was not an adequate time in which a couple should and could judge if their marriage was a failure. Lord Hailsham, the Lord Chancellor, agreed that not a single marriage had been saved by the imposition of a time bar. However, though a practising churchman himself, he said that those members of the Church who had opposed change had 'every right to legislate' for the Church's own communicants. They did not have the right to 'impose their views about marriage' on the 'other kinds of marriage which the state has to celebrate'.

The divorce between church and state is even more clearly established by the Constitution in Australia. Accordingly, the views of the churches and of theologians cannot, in our polity, have a binding effect. Just the same, our culture remains profoundly influenced by the Judaeo-Christian tradition. Even agnostics will gladly look to the churches, their leaders and members for guidance upon the ethical debates of IVF and beyond. It is for that reason that this book is a useful contribution to the literature. There are many who will read these pages and differ from the views expressed. But none may doubt that the questions posed are deserving of the thoughtful reflection of our citizens. At stake is nothing less than the future of humanity.

M. D. KIRBY

Sydney
12 March 1984

1   Australian Law Reform Commission, *Human tissue transplants* (ALRC 7), AGPS, Canberra, 1977.
2   *Hollis* v. *State of Kentucky*, 33 *Criminal Law Rep.* 1005 (1983).
3   *Udale* v. *Bloomsbury Area Health Authority* [1983] 1 WLR 1098.
4   See for example the Morgan Gallup Poll, April 1983, noted E. Weisberg, 'Report from Fertility Society of Australia Second Scientific Meeting', in *Healthright,* vol. 3, no. 2, February 1984, pp. 33, 35.

1

The ethics of IVF: where the debate is

Oliver Heyward

As is often the case with dramatic advances in technology the community was taken unawares by the announcement of the development of successful techniques in what has become known as 'in vitro fertilisation'. Ethical, legal, social and economic questions were immediately raised, and a vigorous debate has developed in the media and in learned journals of many kinds.

It is the intention of the Social Responsibilities Commission of the Anglican Church of Australia to draw together in this book some responses to these questions at this point in the debate. These have been provided by some of the members of the Commission itself and by others who have been invited to do so because of their particular involvement in the issue. To them we express our thanks for their willingness to share in what we hope will be a useful contribution from Christian perspectives.

One thing that has become clear since the debate became public is that the ethical questions relate to much more than the techniques of in vitro fertilisation. For this reason we prefer to use the wider term 'reproductive technology'.

For the Social Responsibilties Commission itself the debate began early in December 1981. From that first consideration it was evident that Christians face a real dilemma in trying to assess the moral implications of what is being done. The essential question is: at what stage does human life begin?

For many Christians there can be no debate. Human life begins at the moment that the sperm is joined to the ovum, and the embryo thus formed must be treated with the full respect accorded to a human being. Those who take this view are also those who oppose absolutely the use of abortion, which they see as the taking of human life. They are generally also opposed to the use of artificial means of contraception, which they see as the frustration of God's appointed way of creating life.

There is, however, another body of Christian opinion which holds that an embryo consisting of a small number of cells has the potential to become a human being, but is not actually so until its development is further advanced. On this view embryos fertilised 'in vitro' which are in excess of what is required to achieve a successful pregnancy may be discarded, or frozen for subsequent use. The difficulty with this position is the impossibility of defining with any accuracy the point in its development when an embryo ceases to be a collection of cells and becomes a human being. None of the attempts that have been made to define this point have found general acceptance.

For those who hold the latter view in vitro fertilisation is morally acceptable under certain conditions, as also is contraception, and even abortion where the survival of the mother is in conflict with that of the child at a very early stage in its development.

At its meeting in December 1981 the Commission understood the new reproductive technology to be still experimental, and called for 'clear ethical guidelines to be established by law within which all biomedical experiments should proceed'. Its public statement went on: 'We express in the strongest terms our grave concern at experiments with human life forms without any debate of the ethical issues involved and without legal limits'. It then listed a number of areas of experimentation requiring further debate, including artificial insemination by donor, in vitro fertilisation, impregnation from a frozen embryo, surrogate mothers, and screening of foetuses to ensure 'normality' by amniocentesis.

Papers were prepared by several members of the Commission for its next meeting in May. An extended debate made even clearer the division of ethical principle outlined above. In the outcome the following resolution was passed by a majority vote:

> We consider that the use of the procedure of IVF may be ethically acceptable, in the case of childless married couples who cannot have children by other means.
>
> Pending the formation of a fully informed Christian viewpoint on all that the process involves, we advance the following guidelines:
>
> (i) IVF and ET should be available only to married couples.

(ii) Sperm and ova must be from the couple.

(iii) Fertilisation of embryos should be restricted to such number of ova as are necessary to accomplish a successful pregnancy.

(iv) Professional counselling should be provided both before and after participating in the program.

(v) An abnormal child should not be aborted as a matter of course and amniocentesis therefore should not be compulsory as part of the program.

(vi) Experimentation beyond IVF and ET should not be permitted with human embryos: specifically cloning, genetic engineering, artificial placentae, surrogate motherhood, human–animal hybrids, embryo freezing.

Also in May 1982 the Government of Victoria, where world leadership in the IVF process had been achieved, set up a committee under the Chairmanship of Professor P. L. Waller. Its terms of reference were 'to consider the social, ethical and legal issues arising from in vitro fertilisation'. Its Interim Report issued in September 1982 included among its recommendations that 'pending its further report or reports . . . the IVF program be limited to cases in which the gametes are obtained from husband and wife and the embryos are transferred into the uterus of the wife; and admission to the IVF program is preceded, accompanied and followed by appropriate counselling'.

At its meeting in November 1982 the Commission addressed itself to the question of artificial insemination by donor. This followed a major principle developed in our consideration of IVF; that is, that used within the context of marriage reproductive technology can be morally acceptable. It can be seen simply as helping to overcome a physical disability which produces infertility.

Once either sperm or ovum from a third party is introduced, or even an embryo where neither sperm nor ovum come from the couple concerned, then a radically different situation exists. In a statement issued in February 1983 the Commission said:

> The Commission is not able to recommend AID because of the Christian understanding of marriage as an exclusive relationship between husband and wife. While we recognise that there is no adulterous intent involved in the process of AID it nevertheless involves the intrusion of a third party into the intimate sphere of the marital state as represented by his sperm, i.e. his reproductive capacity.

It was for this reason that the statement began: 'This Commission believes that AID is inconsistent with Christian moral tradition and cannot therefore recommend it'. However the statement went on:

> Recognising that AID has been operating for some years and may well continue, we recommend the following guidelines for its future operation:

(i) AID should be available only to married couples, in line with the recommendations on IVF in the Interim Report of the Victorian government inquiry into IVF. Single women and lesbian couples should be specifically excluded.

(ii) AID children should be told of their true origins because deception is damaging to both parents and the child. Donors should sign a contract to make their identity available to children who might seek them out. Hospitals should be prohibited from destroying donor records.

(iii) All aspects of AID should be covered by law, consistent in all States, and compatible with laws on IVF. Such laws should cover fatherhood, custodial rights, inheritance of property, quality of donor sperm, payment of donors, preservation of genetic information, and the right of a child to know its origins.

(iv) Legislation should provide for removal of the present ex-nuptial status and other legal handicap applying to AID children.

(v) As with IVF, professional counselling should be available before, during and after the process, consistent with the laws applying to legal adoption.

In this statement the Commission made specific its understanding of some of the legal and social problems arising from the use of this reproductive technology. These problems arise as soon as the technology is used outside a marital relationship.

April 1983 saw the publication of an Issues Paper on *Donor gametes in IVF* by the Waller committee in Victoria. This paper considered at greater depth the problems which had caused concern to the Commission. It stated that the problems raised by AID and IVF are virtually the same.

Under the heading of 'Psychological and social implications' the Issues Paper makes the following point:

A basal principle needs to be established: whose interests should be paramount? In all legislation affecting children in family life, such as the *Family Law Act 1975,* the interests of the child are said to be paramount. This expresses a value obviously held central in our community.

One thing seems clear, however, and that is that in the development of all aspects of reproductive technology the prime consideration has been the satisfaction of the desire for a child on the part of those who are infertile.

In all its statements the Commission has highlighted the need to consider the interests of the child to be born as a result of the processes being used. Up to date no statement of government policy seems to have taken up this point adequately.

In Victoria the Government in a statement of intended legislation, while dealing fully with the legal problems, has not really come to terms with this question. It is to be hoped that the legislation when ultimately brought down will do so.

At its meeting in May 1983 the Commission, responding to the Issues Paper of the Victorian government inquiry, made one further specific contribution, calling for a limit on the freezing of embryos in the IVF program:

> If there is to be any freezing, the Commission as a whole believes that the number of eggs fertilised in the IVF process should be kept to a minimum, and the freezing of embryos should only take place where the intention is to implant the embryo in the womb of the biological mother. It is the conviction of some members of the Commission that freezing of embryos should not take place at all, because of the possible damage caused to the embryo by the freezing process and the problems associated with excess embryos.

In this statement as in others the initial Christian dilemma is again seen. However the work of the Commission does show that while strongly differing positions are held within the one group it is still possible to formulate guidelines which can be of assistance to the wider community.

Obviously the Anglican Social Responsibilities Commission has not been the only Christian body addressing itself to these questions. I have quoted at length from its statements in order to show the process of its thinking, and to give a sample of how such a process works.

Other contributors to this book will show how the ethical problems have been considered by secular committees such as the Ethics Committee of the Queen Victoria Medical Centre, of which Professor William Walters is a member, and the Victorian government committee as seen by Dr John Henley. We have also sought opinions on these matters from representatives of other disciplines such as Professor Gareth Jones and Dr Ditta Bartels.

From within the Commission itself we have asked for an elaboration of the two main Christian approaches to which I have already referred. Dr John Morgan and the Rev. John Fleming have both written and spoken widely on these issues. We have also sought comment on some of the legal issues from another member of the Commission, Mr F. J. Brown. The effects of decisions on these matters on the family from the perspective of welfare are considered by the Secretary of the Commission, the Rev. Alan Nichols.

No Christian analysis of any subject would be complete without an examination of the biblical principles involved. Even in a matter of late twentieth century technology these principles still apply, and they are presented by the Rev. Michael Hill. And because the example of

Christ himself points always to the supreme value of the individual human being in the eyes of God the pastoral, caring dimensions of this new technology are considered by the Rev. Roy Bradley.

It is the overall pastoral approach that has been the prime consideration of the Commission. The legal implications are vital and must form the basis of any action taken by government to control the use of the technology. For a Christian group it is the effects of what is done and upon the people concerned that are most important. In particular our concern has been to ensure that the interests of the children are protected.

This is made clear by the following extract from a submission made to the Victorian government inquiry, prepared for the Commission by Dr John Morgan:

> Children are valued in and for themselves, being usually conceived and born within permanent and affective relationships on the part of the biological and social parents. The marital relationship is also enhanced by children.
>
> Because it appears to be the case that children are best brought up within a permanent and stable relationship, one that is to a degree guaranteed by the formal commitment to permanency of a relationship, the Social Responsibilities Commission thinks that the best interests of all would be served by IVF being restricted to use within childless marriages
> . . .
> The restriction that genetic materials should come from the husband and wife, who will also be the social parents, is related to the desire to protect present values, and also to act in the best interests of children so conceived and born.
>
> The opposition of the Commission to AID is obviously related to many different points but includes such concerns as the relationship between biological and social identity, and the interest of the child in terms of the desire to know and understand one's past history.

This present volume has been prepared by and on behalf of the Social Responsibilities Commission of the Anglican Church of Australia as a contribution to the continuing debate on the new reproductive technology. Decisions are being made by governments, laws are being drafted to control its use. Much public debate has already taken place, but more is required. The ethical issues involved are of fundamental importance to the structure of our society. The effects of what is being done today will be felt for generations to come.

I commend the book to you, its readers, in the hope that it will stimulate your thinking on these questions, so that you may make your own contribution to the continuing debate in the wider community.

2

IVF technology and its major ethical implications

William A. W. Walters

In vitro fertilisation (IVF) and embryo transfer (ET) were developed initially in the human to overcome infertility due to pathologically damaged and obstructed oviducts (Fallopian tubes). The term in vitro fertilisation means fertilisation in laboratory glassware outside the female genital tract, while embryo transfer is defined as removal of the early embryo from a laboratory container to the uterine cavity of the woman who provided the egg or to that of another woman.

The indications for IVF

Normally, fertilisation of the human egg occurs in the outer part of the oviduct after sperm have ascended the female genital tract from their site of deposition in the vagina. This union of male and female reproductive cells cannot occur if the oviducts are obstructed. Previously, no successful treatment for infertility was available for women whose oviducts could not be repaired surgically. In the light of several years experience with IVF, it is now apparent that it can be used for the treatment of other forms of infertility such as some types of male infertility and idiopathic infertility (infertility of unknown cause).

Further applications of the technique for the management of infertility might include:

(1) the fertilisation in vitro of eggs donated from another woman by sperm of the husband of the recipient, who would have

absent or abnormal ovaries and would therefore be unable to produce her own eggs; and

(2) the fertilisation in vitro of eggs obtained from a woman with an absent or abnormal uterus and transfer of the embryos so produced to the uterus of a surrogate (substitute) mother who would bear the child and surrender it to the egg donor immediately after delivery.

Furthermore, while being a far cry from the treatment of infertility, it is possible that in the future IVF technology could lead to developments such as sex selection, cloning or asexual reproduction, resulting in offspring with a genetic constitution identical with that of the progenitor, ectogenesis or growth of the embryo and foetus entirely outside the female genital tract, and human–animal hybridisation.

Since the birth of Louise Brown, the first child resulting from IVF, in England in 1978 and the birth of the world's second IVF child, Candice Reed, in Melbourne in 1980, well over 100 IVF babies have been born around the world and many more pregnancies are in progress. After the initial success in England and Australia, many centres in Europe, the United States and elsewhere have now adopted IVF technology for the treatment of infertile patients. Thus the procedure can no longer be regarded as experimental but as a standard clinical treatment.

The IVF procedure

Basically, IVF, as currently used for infertility treatment, bypasses the function of the oviduct. It entails:

(1) egg collection from the ovary by a surgical technique termed laparoscopy;

(2) sperm collection by masturbation;

(3) the bringing together of egg and sperm cells after suitable preparation to achieve fertilisation and embryo formation;

(4) embryo maturation in culture medium in the laboratory;

(5) transfer of the early two- to four-cell embryo to the uterine cavity, where it has about a 40 per cent chance of embedding successfully in the lining of the uterus compared with the natural process.[1]

In order to increase the prospects for successful IVF pregnancy, the ovaries are stimulated to produce more than the usual one egg per cycle by oral administration of a drug called Clomiphene. Consequently, several eggs can be collected at the time of laparoscopy, fertilised, and subsequently transferred to the uterus and/or stored by cryopreservation. The latter is essentially a freezing process which, like deep freeze refrigeration, allows embryos to be preserved indefinitely in a state of suspended animation. When they are required for implantation they can be thawed and transferred to the uterine cavity by a catheter in the usual way.

The scope for IVF

It is estimated that about 30 000 to 40 000 couples in Australia are infertile as a result of tubal disease and that another 5000 to 10 000 couples have infertility of unknown cause.[2] Thus the scope for IVF treatment in Australia is extensive.

The morality of IVF

IVF and ET used to overcome the problem of infertility would seem to be in the best tradition of medicine by relieving a form of human suffering. However, because they involve manipulation of human life in its earliest developmental stages, they have given rise, understandably, to much concern about the future of human reproduction and human life as we know it.

They highlight questions about the nature of human life: When does it begin? When is it actually as opposed to potentially human? What are the characteristics that distinguish human life from other forms of life?

Furthermore, they stimulate thought about moral questions such as: Is it right to tamper with reproduction in this way? Could human life as we know it be threatened with extinction? Is man trying to play God? Are we likely to see these techniques being developed in an immoral manner?

The main ethical issues

At this stage, it might be useful to outline the major ethical problems arising from IVF technology. Because of the nature of ethics it is not possible to arrive at answers to these problems which would be universally acceptable to members of the community. However, a discussion of the problems helps us to ask the right questions concerning our motives, decisions and actions so that we may be rationally self-conscious about them and act responsibly. In the western world, the moral teachings of the Judaeo-Christian religious traditions have provided the basis for ethical behaviour, but their influence in this regard, especially in education, appears to be declining. In future, the teaching of morality and ethics may have a largely secular basis. Nevertheless, for the theist the heart of religion is the divine presence, the awareness of which will be the determinative factor in any distinctively religious understanding of ethics, as pointed out by Macquarrie (1966).[3]

The moral status of the embryo

The moral status of the embryo has emerged as probably the most important ethical issue associated with IVF. In particular, discussion centres around when the embryo is to be regarded as a person with full human rights and what factors determine personhood. Indeed, some distinguished moral theologians and biologists have come to regard personhood as the key issue raised by IVF that requires further analysis.

Four differing perceptions of the moral status of the human embryo can be discerned:

(1) It may be regarded in the way that a fully developed adult human being is regarded.

(2) It may be regarded as a piece of tissue or a discrete human organ.

(3) It may be thought of as a lower animal.

(4) It may be viewed as occupying a relatively unique moral category in which its status is close to but not identical with that of a typical adult human being.

In the United States, the National Commission for the Protection of Human Subjects of Biomedical and Behavioural Research has adopted the fourth perception of the embryo or foetus, in that it views human life at this stage neither as a person nor as an object, but rather as a potential person.[4] As such, the embryo or foetus must be shown due respect by refraining from actions that would violate its dignity and integrity. In other words, our action should be directed towards fostering the well-being of each individual embryo or foetus and minimising harm. While we must respect the authority of a pregnant woman to have an abortion, we are not to encourage abortions.[4]

In Australia the National Health and Medical Research Council Medical Research Ethics Committee has drawn attention to a wide variety of viewpoints about the status of the human foetus.[5] At one end of the spectrum are those who believe that the foetus is a human being from the earliest stage of its development, and at the other extreme are those who assert that the foetus does not become a human person until it is born alive and lives independently outside its mother's body. Some of these would say that until the foetus becomes an actual person it is an object or a non-personal organism which has value only insofar as it is wanted by its progenitors. The Committee suggested that there would probably be few people in the Australian community who would take either of these positions without qualification and therefore believed that neither of them should provide the basis for public policy. Rather the Committee sought to avoid violating philosophical values which it thought were widely accepted in the Australian community while at the same time avoiding contradicting demonstrable biological facts. In other words, it took the middle course and came to much the same conclusion as did the United States Committee.

Grobstein, a biologist and former President of the American Academy of Sciences, believes that the nature of personhood (or self) is inextricably linked with activities and processes within the brain.[6] He points out that before 7 to 8 weeks of age, the embryo lacks a completely developed brain and has not yet elaborated the necessary connections among nerve cells to enable the higher brain areas concerned with features of sentience (the ability to feel, to respond to stimuli and to be aware of the environment) to function.

For the most part, the Judaeo-Christian tradition has ascribed a high value to prenatal human life based upon theories of ensoulment or animation, on the one hand, and a concern for the protection of innocent life on the other. During the last two centuries most theologians have been convinced by the discoveries of biologists that the human principle of life is given at fertilisation. Now that purely mechanistic ideas in biology have given way to a more holistic concept of what it means to be a human being there is, I believe, a need to look at the problem afresh. In this regard it is interesting that Häring[7] and Dunstan[8], Catholic and Anglican moral theologians respectively, see merit in reconsidering what is meant by hominisation and ensoulment in the course of embryonic development. Häring's personal opinion is that hominisation is probably dependent on the development of the cerebral cortex and that before days 25 to 40 after fertilisation the brain has not developed sufficiently for the embryo to be considered a human person. Perhaps surprisingly in the circumstances, this view is remarkably consistent with that of the biologist, Grobstein.[6] It is also consistent with the ancient Hebrew idea of the soul being a concept of a personally experienced reality[9], which can only occur when the brain is present and functioning.

It is important to realise that the human embryo resulting from IVF is only grown in the laboratory for 36 to 48 hours until it has divided into two to four cells, when it is then transferred to the uterus of the biological mother or preserved by freezing for subsequent transfer to the uterus. At this stage, the embryo consisting of a few cells is barely visible to the naked eye and shows no human characteristics whatsoever under the microscope: it is merely a cluster of cells with appearances similar to those of other body cells.

The question is often asked: What happens when more than one egg is obtained from a woman and fertilised in the laboratory? This would result in more than one embryo, and if only one or two embryos are transferred to the women's uterus, what happens to the others? Can they be discarded or used for experimental purposes or must all of them be preserved for future transfer to the uterus?

Cryopreservation offers the advantages of allowing excess embryos to be stored:

(1) For use in subsequent cycles in the same woman should the first attempt at embryo transfer fail. In this way, further surgical procedures and a general anaesthetic to collect eggs could be avoided and the excess embryos would not die, which would otherwise happen if they were kept for longer than 7−10 days in ordinary culture media.

(2) When not wanted by the progenitors and subsequently donated to another infertile couple.

(3) For other special reasons that might indicate embryo storage in individual cases.

Cryopreservation and subsequent thawing and implantation of embryos with normally progressing pregnancies have now been reported in the human.[10] Ethically, concern has been expressed that the technique might lead to an increase in the abortion rate or an increased incidence of foetal abnormalities. The evidence from animal studies suggests that pregnancies following cryopreservation of embryos have the same viability and incidence of foetal anomalies as do pregnancies resulting from non-frozen embryos.[11,12] Cryopreservation also raises the question of ownership of embryos. Once the embryo is in a hospital embryo bank, to whom does it belong? If it is regarded as a human life, can one human being own another human being? If the donors of the original sperm and egg cells die prematurely, who decides what happens to the embryo? How long should embryos be kept in a frozen state? If the germ cell donors do not want their frozen embryo and do not want to donate it to another infertile couple, can it be used for research purposes or discarded? Obviously, the answer to such questions will depend upon one's personal view of the moral status of the embryo.

As far as the Queen Victoria Medical Centre is concerned ethical guidelines[13] for clinicians and scientists involved in IVF include statements to the effect that parents must give the medical and scientific staff their informed consent to any procedure that may be undertaken on the embryo and that when excess normal embryos have been produced as a result of IVF, those that are not transferred to the uterus should be preserved by freezing rather than using them for experimentation or discarding them.

Informed consent by participants

Generally, the participants in IVF will be a married couple who will produce the eggs and sperm. As is the case with all medical procedures, the intending parents-to-be are given a complete explanation of what is involved and are asked to consider this, ask any questions which they might have, and sign a consent form which provides for either partner withdrawing from the program of treatment at any stage.

Superficially, this type of informed consent appears to be a straightforward matter. The right of every person to reproduce is clearly stated in the Universal Declaration of Human Rights (Geneva, 1948)[14] and the doctor's role in the relief of suffering, of which infertility is one manifestation, has been recognised since ancient times. However, further analysis reveals that the consent is not as straightforward as would appear at first sight because the adult participants are consenting to a proposed action which is not centred on themselves but on the embryo and child-to-be. Ramsey (1970)[15] argues that there is no meaning to the concept of consent under these circumstances and that non-therapeutic (from the embryo's aspect) experiments or procedures designed for the benefit of others (the IVF parents) would constitute a wrong. The embryo is seen to be similar to the child or incompetent adult who has no freedom of choice in the matter. May (1977)[16], in drawing attention to the risk of harm to the embryo as a result of IVF, believes that the intending parents are jeopardising the interests of the embryo for their own interests to have a child. Others, however, regard informed consent by the prospective parents to relate not only to their right to procreate, but also to their needs, namely to have a child. Fletcher (1976)[17] argues that human needs have priority over embryo rights and that by consenting to IVF potential parents are embarking upon a responsible planned parenthood in contrast to leaving things to the whims of nature, as is the case with normal procreation.

If IVF is extended to include the eggs or sperm donated by a third party or implantation of the embryo in the uterus of a woman who is not the egg donor, consent to what is done with the donated reproductive cells or transferred embryo introduces the question of the consent of the third party. Should the reproductive cell donor or host mother have any rights of consent in determining what might be done with the embryo or child? It might be argued that the rules governing adoption of a child could also apply in these circumstances, but the matter still requires clarification.

There is no doubt that most clinicians using IVF have seen their main task as one of attempting to satisfy the infertile couple in their quest for a child. However, Daniel (1982)[18] has urged clinicians to try to look at the problem from the child's point of view as well. Instead of insisting on the right of a couple to have a child, we should also bear in mind the right of a child to have parents and, by implication, loving and caring parents. Perhaps, it is argued, not all infertile couples will provide a favourable psychological and physical environment for the rearing of a child. Indeed, some would go even further and suggest that when the desire to have children becomes so overwhelming, it is really an abnormal state of mind, and that it might not be in the best interests of any future child to be born into such an environment. In other words, perhaps the overwhelming desire of some to have a child represents a manifestation of a psychological disorder rather than a genuine desire to provide for the interests of a child. McCormick (1981)[19] is also concerned about the child-to-be and has likened it in some situations as a 'consumer item' to be obtained at all costs. For these reasons, it has been suggested that some form of psychological assessment should be incorporated into the screening of potential patients for IVF, especially as clinicians intervene in a crucial manner to aid conception and therefore presumably have a greater moral responsibility for the embryo and child than in the case of normal conception in which they are not involved.

Marriage and the family

Because IVF is controlled by the intervention of a third party in a laboratory environment outside the realm of bodily love and sexual intercourse, in contrast with the unplanned random nature of normal conception, it is held by some to be dehumanising. Indeed, Ramsey (1975)[20] believes that because procreation is separated from the physical and psychological act of love, the very structure of marriage and the family is threatened, with grave implications for society as a whole.

On the other hand, proponents of IVF argue that the conception has all the features of being intensely human, as it results in a planned and wanted pregnancy which has been brought about not as a consequence of unthinking sexual desire but as a culmination of much love, concern and preparation by the intending parents. Fletcher (1974)[21] has gone further to suggest that, in IVF, man is sharing with God in his continually evolving creation, even in the creation of man himself.

The individual conceived by IVF

Concern has been expressed that IVF may result in a greater risk of abnormality developing in the embryo, with an increased risk of subsequent miscarriage or birth of an abnormal baby. These possibilities are speculative and cannot yet be proved or disproved until a larger number of babies conceived by IVF have been born. However, all the indications from animal studies[22] and from human data[1] already available are that IVF is unlikely to be accompanied by a significant increase in foetal abnormalities.

It has also been suggested that the individual conceived by IVF, when learning later in life about the nature of his or her conception, might suffer from adverse psychological effects. He or she might feel unable to identify with others conceived naturally or might feel antagonistic to those responsible for his or her creation, and consequently might find it difficult to become integrated into society as a useful citizen. Once again, this is entirely speculative. Presumably the love and affection with which such a child would be reared would mitigate against the development of such adverse psychological effects. To some extent, adopted children are in a similar situation and yet rarely grow up to be misfits in society provided they have had the benefits of a loving family environment. It must also be appreciated that resentment towards or even rejection of parents and other antisocial behaviour can be expressed by children who were conceived naturally.

Individual versus community needs

In Australia it is estimated that the annual running costs of an IVF program dealing with up to fifteen procedures a week amount to about $100 000. At present only 10 to 15 per cent of procedures result in successful pregnancy.[23] Therefore, some members of the community question whether it is morally justifiable to provide sophisticated medical services of this kind for a minority in the population when there are urgent community needs of a more general nature affecting a much greater proportion of people. On the other hand, should the minority have to suffer just because they are in a minority group? Indeed, it might be argued that the rapidly increasing knowledge accruing as a result of IVF will eventually benefit the entire community in terms of more efficient reproduction and family planning. Furthermore, increasing knowledge of cellular growth and function as a result of IVF technology may help in the prevention and treatment of congenital abnormalities, ageing and cancer.

If facilities are not provided to treat all infertile people who might benefit from IVF, how should patients be selected for treatment? If selective criteria are used, how are they to be decided upon? Or should the selection be made entirely on a random basis? Three positions may be discerned:

(1) The all or none principle: if all patients cannot receive equal treatment then no patient should be treated, since to treat some at the expense of others is morally wrong.

(2) Selection of some patients could be made by application of medical and utilitarian standards.

(3) Random selection could be used to eliminate criteria based upon general social worth.

Yezzi (1980)[24] draws attention to three issues that are particularly relevant in making decisions about the allocation of health care resources: prospects of treatment effectiveness, the role of social worth, and the moral acceptability of random selection.

We have not solved this problem in our own clinic, which has a two- to three-year waiting list. At present, all patients suitable for IVF are treated in chronological order of presentation, providing that they have no concomitant systemic disease requiring prior therapy.

As the cost of health care in the western world is rapidly escalating, this very question of the allocation of scarce medical resources is becoming one of the major ethical problems demanding solution.

A United States study[1] has estimated that the total cost to the patient for an initial IVF treatment is about $7500, with each additional attempt at pregnancy amounting to $5000. At current levels of efficacy, estimated from overall published data at roughly 10 per cent for a given laparoscopy, something of the order of $38 000 would be required to ensure a roughly 50 per cent chance of live birth for a particular patient. For each child born, the estimated aggregate costs are about $50 000, borne by both the successful and unsuccessful couples. The same study concludes that it is not unreasonable to anticipate that the overall efficacy could double, thereby providing a significant economic saving as well as reducing discomfort and inconvenience for patients. If this improved efficacy was achieved it would make IVF economically advantageous when compared with more complicated types of tubal surgery.

Future possibilities

The success of IVF undoubtedly paves the way for related techniques such as determination of sex, pre-implantation genetic screening of embryos and repair of genetic defects, cloning, ectogenesis, and human–animal hybridisation. None of these has yet been attempted in man but it may not be long before proposals are made to extend research into at least some of these areas. The associated ethical problems should therefore be explored before proposals come forward to find the community unprepared to deal with them.

It is understandable that the possibility of these future developments terrifies many people, who see in them the eventual destruction of the human species. Hence the repeated calls for an end to or at least a moratorium on human reproductive cell and embryo research. Such critics of IVF, while reluctantly acknowledging its benefits in the relief of infertility, feel that this is far outweighed by the potential dangers. They adhere to the 'slippery slope' or 'thin edge of the wedge' hypothesis that the beginning of such research inevitably leads to its further extension, resulting in undesirable consequences. Proponents of IVF challenge this hypothesis by citing many examples of man embracing the beginnings of a new technology without allowing it to be developed to his detriment. In other words, it is not the technology that is inherently good or bad but how man chooses to use it.

It might be useful to consider briefly some of the ethical implications of these possible future developments.

1   Determination of sex

Parental selection of sex based on the desire for a child of a particular sex or to avoid a hereditary disorder manifested in one sex raises two ethical issues. Firstly, the sex ratio of the population might become grossly imbalanced, with adverse social consequences. Secondly, presumably embryos of the sex not desired would be discarded or donated to other prospective parents, which would raise ethical objections based upon the moral status of the embryo.

2   Pre-implantation genetic screening and repair of genetic defects

Early embryos could be examined for chromosome abnormalities and genetic defects and, if such were found, the embryos could either be discarded or an attempt could be made to repair the genetic defect. Here ethical discussion centres around the potential risks and benefits of the various techniques and on the alternatives of the repair versus the discard of defective early embryos.

3 Cloning

Cloning is the process whereby an egg cell can be fertilised by the nucleus of a body cell other than the sperm cell. Theoretically, in the laboratory the nucleus of a cell from any of the body cells (excluding the reproductive cells) could be introduced into the human egg cell, after its own nucleus had been removed or destroyed. The egg cell would then have the full human complement of forty-six chromosomes and would start to behave as if it had been fertilised by a sperm. It would start to develop into an embryo and ultimately into another human being. The essential difference in this mode of reproduction would be that this particular human being would have precisely the same genetic constitution as that of the person who donated the cell nucleus. Furthermore, the donor of the egg would not be contributing genetically to the future offspring unless one of her own body cell nuclei was used to fertilise her own egg. Thus, cloning is an asexual form of reproduction and can even do away with the absolute necessity of a male factor.

It must be emphasised that while cloning has been used with varying success in frogs, salamanders and fruit flies, it has not yet been successful in higher animals or man.

Another type of cloning is embryo fission. This involves separating the cells of an early embryo at the two-cell stage and transplanting each of them into a recipient uterus, suitably primed hormonally, where they can develop into complete and genetically identical embryos. This technique has been applied to mouse embryos with success.[25]

Cloning might result in the offspring eventually knowing that he or she has the same genetic potential as an identifiable progenitor. If multiple copies of this one progenitor were created it might lead to a loss of the sense of identity in the offspring. Furthermore, should these offspring reproduce sexually, the risk of an increased incidence of genetic defects in the progeny would be serious. Perhaps of most concern, however, is the power that cloning would give to selected members of the present generation to determine the genetic characteristics of future human beings. Who should decide about the criteria for cloning and what criteria would one select for? It is probably the power that cloning would give to selected members of the present generation to determine the genetic characteristics of future human life that would raise objections from many members of the community.

On the credit side, cloning could be employed to allow women who cannot produce egg cells or men who cannot produce sperm, by donating one or more of their body cell nuclei for introduction into a donated egg, to contribute to the production of children. Cloning might also be an advantage if it became necessary to reproduce specialised individuals with characteristics for fulfilling unique roles in the community in unusual situations, e.g. in the case of nuclear war or space travel.

If one partner in a marriage had a severe hereditary defect, cloning with the other partner's genetic material would avoid the defect being transmitted to any offspring. Indeed, cloning might be necessary in future to complement sexual reproduction as part of any program aimed at preventing deterioration of the human gene pool.

Probably one of the most important arguments in favour of cloning is that it would allow the study of factors responsible for cell growth, multiplication and differentiation. In turn, this might lead to a better understanding of and cure for cancer and infant malformations. Cloning would also allow study of the ageing process in cells, with the possibility of diminishing the rate of ageing and increasing the human life span. It could also lead to a better understanding of immunological responses of the body and thereby have application to the management of allergies, wound healing and organ transplantation. However, such studies would entail experimentation with the early embryo and might be opposed on the grounds of interference with human life and the possible production of abnormal embryos. In both situations the embryos might have to be destroyed, and this would meet with strong moral objections by some.

4 Ectogenesis

Ectogenesis is the term applied to growth of the embryo entirely outside the uterus. This occurs briefly during the procedure of IVF, when immediately after fertilisation the very early embryo consisting of two cells is grown in a medium in the laboratory. Here, ectogenesis will be used to refer to the entire growth and development of the foetus outside the uterine environment in the laboratory. This is not as far fetched as it may sound because very small premature babies are already being kept alive in incubators in neonatal intensive care nurseries. Furthermore, they can survive and develop normally. Although an artificial placenta has not yet been successfully designed to support foetal life, the time is not far off when an embryo might be encouraged to grow and develop throughout foetal life to maturity entirely outside the uterus.

Ectogenesis might allow women with various diseases to produce children without a threat to their lives. For example, women with poorly controlled drug-resistant high blood pressure in whom normal pregnancy would cause a deterioration might be better served by opting for ectogenesis rather than attempting intrauterine pregnancy. Similarly, in women who have had recurrent miscarriages, where it has been established that the foetuses have been normal in development and where no obvious cause for the failure of the pregnancies has been found, ectogenesis might provide the solution to a barren marriage and the psychological trauma of repeated pregnancy loss.

Ethically, providing that the procedure does not interfere with normal foetal growth and development, the main objection to ectogenesis is that it would be so far removed from normal human nurturing that it might have a dehumanising effect. As the parent or parents would have much less contact with the foetus than in normal intrauterine pregnancy, adverse psychological effects may occur in them and in the child. Moreover, there might be a tendency for those in charge of the nurturing machinery to become so familiar with it that they lose reverence for human life. On the other hand, it could be argued that the above speculations are fallacious in the light of the knowledge we have about parenting of premature babies, who may have to be cared for in incubators in neonatal intensive care nurseries for periods of several months continuously. Under these circumstances the parents are encouraged to spend as much time as possible in the nursery with their babies and to identify closely with them. There is no evidence that parents or babies suffer adversely psychologically if close contact of this type is maintained throughout the babies' stay in the nursery.

Another argument in favour of ectogenesis is that total extrauterine development would eliminate maternal morbidity and mortality associated with intrauterine pregnancy and would avoid possible birth trauma to both mother and foetus. Indeed, if the environment could be closely controlled without adverse side effects in the extrauterine situation, some foetal malformations associated with agents circulating in the mother, e.g. drugs such as alcohol and tobacco and infective agents, might be prevented altogether. In other words, one might speculate that prospective parents would be able to protect their offspring better in a perfect artificial environment than in the natural intrauterine one, exposed as it is to many adverse influences that cannot always be readily avoided in modern urban civilisation.

Some feminists[26] would favour ectogenesis as they see childbirth as being a barbaric event causing temporary deformation of the body, pain and discomfort.

5 *Human—animal hybrids*

In future it might be possible to create human—animal hybrids by inserting human genetic material into the egg cell of an animal and so produce a man—animal hybrid. If such a procedure was attempted it would be more likely to achieve success using the egg cells of primates because of their closer relationship to human beings on the evolutionary scale.

It is not surprising that this topic more than any other engenders alarm, revulsion and fear amongst most people. Nevertheless, the Protestant moral theologian Fletcher[27] has put forward the view that man—animal hybrids could be morally justified if they were able to protect human beings from danger, disease or unpleasant occupations. Whilst they would be of lower intelligence than man, they would be able to carry out unpleasant work and mundane tasks in the community, relieving man for more skilled occupations. Nevertheless, Edwards[28] probably echoes the sentiments of most of us when he states that such hybridisation would be condemning the human component to a condition unworthy of it.

Perhaps the ancient Greek myth of the minotaur, which was a man—bull hybrid, is relevant to this discussion. It was so dreadful to look upon that it had to be closed away in a labyrinth.

Resolution of ethical problems

If the community, including the clinicians and scientists, ignore ethical implications of IVF and its possible future developments this means that they have, in fact, made a decision to evade the complicated moral, legal, social and economic consequences of such procedures. They would also be ignoring the concerns of those in the community who have expressed opposition to IVF. Both would be irresponsible decisions and unworthy of the best traditions of medicine.

In Melbourne, the ethical issues raised by IVF were discussed with the hospital and Monash University Ethics Committees at the very beginning of work in this area. At the same time members of the IVF team attempted to increase public awareness and discussion of the issues by talking to media representatives and various groups in the community. After initial approval for IVF to proceed at the Queen Victoria Medical Centre, a Centre for Human Bioethics was established at Monash University and at subsequent ethical discussions advice from the staff of this centre was solicited. Nevertheless, despite these attempts to tap community views and advice it must be conceded, I think, that many of those who subsequently declared their partial or complete opposition to IVF did so without having any idea of the extent to which the medical team had considered and sought expert advice about the ethical issues.

The Monash University team has always advocated the establishment of a completely independent body, consisting of representatives of appropriate disciplines, to consider in depth such issues and then to recommend what action, if any, should be taken by government. If the government approved of the recommendations of such an expert advisory committee, it could, if necessary, pass appropriate legislation to control IVF. In fact, in the State of Victoria the Government established such a committee under the chairmanship of a Law Reform Commissioner, Professor Louis Waller. In 1982 this committee produced its first Interim Report, which advocated approval of IVF for treatment of infertility in married couples. The committee is now considering freeze–thawing of embryos and their transfer to non-donors and will issue a further report on this aspect.in due course.

In the U.S.A. there is a President's Commission for the Study of Ethical Problems in Medicine and Biomedical and Behavioural Research. This is a national body and I believe that there would be many advantages in having a similar national body in this country. Perhaps the Australian Law Reform Commission could serve this function. Indeed, Mr Justice Kirby[29], Chairman of this Commission, has urged Australians to respond to the ethical challenge of IVF and its possible future applications by the words:

> Let it not be the epitaph of our generation that we proved ourselves brilliant in a dazzling field of scientific endeavour but so morally bankrupt and legally incompetent that we could not bother or did not have the courage to sort out the consequences for our society and for the human species.

The Australian Law Reform Commission has already had considerable experience in performing such a function as it prepared a report on the difficult moral, legal and social problems associated with transplantation of human tissues.[30] This report has received much commendation and has been used as a model for other countries.

Individual responsibility and reproduction

A number of prominent medical scientists and biologists have drawn attention to the need for society to reconsider the question of the right of individuals to reproduce. Foremost in this vanguard was Sir Alan Parkes (1969)[31], the distinguished British physiologist who, in discussing the right to reproduce in an overcrowded world, drew up a declaration of human obligations which states:

> It is an obligation of men and women: (1) not to produce unwanted children; (2) not to take a substantial risk of begetting a mentally or physically defective child; (3) not to produce children because of irresponsibility or

religious observance, merely as a byproduct of sexual intercourse; (4) to plan the number and spacing of births in the best of interests of mother, child and the rest of the family; (5) to give the best possible mental and physical environment to the child in its formative years and to produce children therefore only in the course of a loving and stable relationship between man and woman; and (6) however convinced the individual may be of his of her superior qualities, not for this reason to produce children of numbers which if equalled by everyone would be demographically catastrophic.

Birch (1975)[32] in Australia has also argued for a reconsideration of individual freedom to make decisions about reproduction and the need for society to make decisions which will limit the area within which individuals are free to decide. The personal challenge now is to rethink the rights, responsibilities and obligations of the individual in his reproductive behaviour to his partner and to himself, to his family, to his neighbours and to society. Parry (1974)[33] suggests that we must now accept a restriction on our right to reproduce, doing so only when a stable parental home is established in which a child may be successfully reared. He concludes by stating that society must construct a new ethos of social attitudes towards reproduction, child rearing and the family, and its hitherto general commendation of the intrinsic virtue of child bearing. Glass (1975)[34] has gone so far as to say that 'the right of individuals to procreate must give place to a new paramount right: the right of every child to enter life with an adequate physical and mental endowment'.

In the light of the above concerns this would seem to be an appropriate time for our community to rethink the wisdom of the statement in the Universal Declaration of Human Rights regarding the right of every individual to have children. Furthermore, it is becoming increasingly clear that society will need to adopt some consensus of opinion about the moral status of the embryo and foetus since so many interventions in human pregnancy with a view to diagnosis of foetal abnormalities and their treatment will be intimately linked with such a consensus.

With man's increasing knowledge of his own reproduction comes an increased responsibility for that process. It seems to me that man now has two alternatives, either to use that knowledge wisely in control of his own genetic future or to ignore the knowledge and fail to act on it. The latter approach might well lead to genetic suicide. Responsible application of new knowledge inevitably involves the conduct of further research in various aspects of human reproduction and for this reason I believe that it is absolutely essential to have such research conducted in the best possible scientific manner in institutions subject to the most vigorous ethical scrutiny of their work. It is in this area of biomedical ethics that much more attention should be concentrated. As Lerner (1975)[35] has pointed out:

> The ethics of decision making in the contemporary world is not clear, but the development of an effective and just machinery for this purpose, as it concerns individuals and society, should have a high place on mankind's agenda.

Personal viewpoint

As a Christian obstetrician and gynaecologist I hold the view that there is nothing inherently immoral about IVF technology when it is used in a responsible manner for the treatment of infertility and possibly in the future for the prevention or treatment of congenital abnormalities.

As far as the moral status of the embryo is concerned, I think that there is an urgent need to explore the question of when the embryo can be regarded as a person. The reason for this is that the properties of human life are not the same as the properties of persons. A cluster of living human embryonic cells may well be a potential person but at what stage does it become invested with personhood? Answers to these questions would provide some guidance to those concerned with the handling and storage or disposal of human embryos.

Modern medicine has enabled many people with hereditary disorders to survive to reproductive age and this will mean that many will transmit such diseases to their progeny. In this way, the human gene pool will progressively deteriorate. Therefore, I regard it as of the utmost importance that human reproduction be controlled to minimise genetic deterioration. For this reason I would support the development of genetic engineering techniques aimed at prevention, diagnosis or treatment of genetically determined diseases. I would see this as responsible Christian stewardship.

At present I see little scope for the clinical application of cloning and ectogenesis and I would be totally opposed to human–animal hybridisation.

In my opinion it would be best if the ethical questions related to IVF and its possible future developments were considered by an independent impartial body representative of community ethics and attitudes with a view to formulating laws governing the control and use of such biological techniques. Ideally, it would be preferable if this committee was a national one rather than having separate committees in each State. In this way, hopefully, we could ensure that the techniques are used responsibly within limits acceptable to the community.

It is my conviction that man will benefit greatly from the development of new techniques in human reproduction. Like so many gifts, newly acquired knowledge can also be used irresponsibly. It is our duty to see that this does not happen by increasing our awareness and understanding of the ethical issues involved. Hopefully, as a result, the decisions we make will lead to action of a constructive, humanitarian kind that will enhance the lives of future generations.

Acknowledgments

The author wishes to express his gratitude to Professors Carl Wood and John Leeton and Dr Alan Trounson for providing technical information and stimulating discussion about ethical problems arising out of IVF and ET. Acknowledgment of the contributions made by members of the Ethics Committees of the Queen Victoria Medical Centre and Epworth Hospital in discussions of ethical issues is also due.

Ultimately, however, the author accepts all responsibility for opinions expressed in this chapter.

1   C. Grobstein, M. Flower & J. Mendeloff, 'External human fertilization: an evaluation of policy', *Science* 222, 1983, pp. 127–33.

2   E. C. Wood, personal communication.

3   J. Macquarrie, *Principles of Christian theology,* SCM, London, 1966, pp. 444–52.

4   R. J. Levine, *Ethics and regulations of clinical research,* Urban and Schwarzenberg, Baltimore–Munich, 1981, pp. 197–206.

5   National Health and Medical Research Council, Medical Research Ethics Committee report on *Ethics in medical research involving the human fetus and human fetal tissue,* AGPS, Canberra, 1983.

6   C. Grobstein, *From chance to purpose: an appraisal of external human fertilization,* Addison-Wesley, Reading, Massachusetts, 1981, pp. 75–106.

7   B. Häring, *Medical ethics,* St Paul, Slough, England, 1972, pp. 75–85.

8   G. R. Dunstan, *The artifice of ethics,* SCM, London, 1974, pp. 70–2.

9   W. L. King, *Introduction to religion,* Harper and Row, New York, 1968, p. 242.

10 A. Trounson & L. Mohr, 'Human pregnancy following cryopreservation, thawing and transfer of an eight-cell embryo', *Nature* 305, 1983, pp. 707–9.

11 R. R. Maurer, H. Bank & R. E. Staples, 'Pre- and post-natal development of mouse embryos after storage for different periods at cryogenic temperatures', *Biology of Reproduction* 16, 2, 1977, pp. 139–46.

12 Y. Tsunoda & T. Sugie, 'Survival of rabbit eggs preserved in plastic straws in liquid nitrogen', *Journal of Reproduction and Fertility* 49, 1977, pp. 173–4.

13 Queen Victoria Medical Centre Ethical Guidelines for Clinicians and Scientists involved in IVF and ET, in *Test-tube babies,* ed. William A. W. Walters & Peter Singer, Oxford University Press, Melbourne, 1982, pp. 146–7.

14 Universal Declaration of Human Rights, 1948 (Geneva), Article 16, Section I.

15 P. Ramsey, *Patient as person,* Yale University, New Haven, 1970, p. 14.

16 W. E. May, *Franciscan Herald,* Chicago, 1977, pp. 55–9.

17 J. Fletcher, in *Bioethics,* ed. T. A. Shannon, Paulist Press, New York, 1976, pp. 336–68.

18 W. J. Daniel, in *Test-tube babies,* ed. William A. W. Walters & Peter Singer, Oxford University Press, Melbourne, 1982, pp. 71–8.

19 R. A. McCormick, *How brave a new world?,* SCM, London, 1981, pp. 327–35.

20 P. Ramsey, *Fabricated man: the ethics of genetic control,* Yale University, New Haven, 1975, pp. 32–40.

21 J. Fletcher, *The ethics of genetic control: ending reproductive roulette,* Anchor, New York, 1974, pp. 166–8.

22 A. B. Mukherjee, 'Normal progeny from fertilization of mouse oocytes matured in culture and spermatozoa capacitated in vitro', *Nature* 237, 1972, pp. 397–8.

23 E. C. Wood, personal communication.

24 R. Yezzi, *Medical ethics: thinking about unavoidable questions,* Holt, Rinehart and Winston, New York, 1980, pp. 96–108.

25 L. E. Karp, *Genetic engineering: threat or promise,* Nelson-Hall, Chicago, 1976, pp. 161–206.

26 S. Firestone, *The dialectic of sex: the case for feminist revolution,* Bantam Books, New York, 1971, pp. 196–200.

27 J. Fletcher, *The ethics of genetic control: ending reproductive roulette,* Anchor, New York, 1974, pp. 147–87.

28 R. G. Edwards, 'Fertilization of human eggs in vitro: morals, ethics and the law', *Quarterly Review of Biology* 49, 1974, pp. 3–14.

29 M. D. Kirby, Law for test tube man? Address to the Fifth Annual General Meeting of Contributors, Queen Victoria Medical Centre, Melbourne, 1981.

30 Law Reform Commission, *Human tissue transplants* (ALRC 7), AGPS, Canberra, 1977.

31 A. S. Parkes, 'The right to reproduce in an overcrowded world', in *Biology and ethics,* ed. F. J. Ebling, Academic Press, London, 1969, p. 109.

32 C. Birch, 'Genetics and moral responsibility', in *Ethics and the quality of life,* ed. C. Birch & P. Abrecht, Pergamon Press, London, 1975, pp. 6–19.

33 H. B. Parry, *Population and its problems: a plain man's guide,* Oxford University Press, Oxford, 1974, pp. 397–409.

34 B. Glass, 'Ethical problems raised by genetics', in *Genetics and the quality of life,* ed. C. Birch & P. Abrecht, Pergamon Press, London, 1975, pp. 50–8.

35 I. M. Lerner, 'Ethics and the new biology', in *Genetics and the quality of life,* ibid., pp. 20–35.

3

The formulation of social policy: principle versus procedure

John Henley

A call for principles

The committee established by the State of Victoria to consider the social, ethical and legal issues arising from in vitro fertilisation produced an Interim Report that was published in September 1982. Among the responses to the Interim Report was one from the Chairman of the Australian Law Reform Commission, the Hon. Mr Justice M. D. Kirby. He submitted that the committee had not indicated in the Interim Report the guiding principle or principles which led to its recommendations and he challenged the committee to make its basic principles clear in a later report. By so doing, he suggested, the committee would render an important service to all who are concerned about the way public policy on controversial matters is to be determined in a secular society.

Since Mr Justice Kirby made this submission the committee has produced two further documents—an Issues Paper and a *Report on donor gametes in IVF*—and these give no indication of an attempt to meet Mr Justice Kirby's challenge. On the contrary, the committee has continued to couch its recommendations in terms of what it considers 'acceptable' to the Victorian community without saying anything about principles which might serve as criteria of acceptability.[1] This practice can be defended on the pragmatic grounds that the committee was acting under quite a deal of public pressure on the issue of donor gametes and therefore lacked the time to produce a considered statement concerning its guiding principles. I would go further, however, and argue that the committee has been wise to avoid Mr Justice Kirby's challenge. My basic reason is not that it would have been very difficult or even impossible for the committee to have reached agreement on such matters but that it is inappropriate to seek such agreement in a society that is not only secular but, to an extent that few can fully appreciate, plural. In other words, there is such a diversity, and even divergence, of beliefs and values, commitments and aspirations among the groups that comprise a modern western society that serious doubt must be cast on the adequacy of the principle or principles according to which any one group would determine social policy.

The principle of the common good

Certain of the principles that inform the debate about IVF and related matters are inadequate simply because they presuppose a homogeneous and not a plural society. The most obvious is that which conceives the essence of social policy to be the maintenance of the common good by the ruler or sovereign. A fellow member of the committee, the Rev. Dr Francis Harman, refers explicitly to this principle near the end of his Dissenting Statement which is an appendix to the *Report on donor gametes in IVF*. He suggests that 'the common weal' requires many legislative, judicial and administrative determinations that 'cause emotional distress to some' (paragraph 13).[2] The basic trouble with this argument is that in a plural society there is not and cannot be a *common* weal or good. This further means that there can be no body, no ruler or sovereign, who is in a position to determine what is and what makes for such a good. At best, the claim to the contrary is paternalistic, as when Dr Harman refers earlier in his Dissenting Statement to 'the traditional role of the Crown as *parens* patriae' (paragraph 10, my italics). At worst, however, this claim is presumptuous, as when Roman Catholic bishops purport to state what *must* be done for the good of society. The deep offence that such presumption causes to many Protestants is, I consider, an issue that has still to be faced squarely in the ecumenical movement. Some Roman Catholics are showing greater sensitivity, however, and urging caution with regard to IVF on the more modest grounds that society needs to achieve a consensus about controversial and possibly hazardous developments before it permits certain individuals or groups to pursue them.[3] Dr Harman makes use of this principle, and also betrays its connection with that relating to the common good, when he appears to base his argument against the use of donor gametes in IVF on the claim that 'the *community* is far from being of *one mind* on a procedure which is essentially a *community* concern' (paragraph 4, my italics).

The principle of consensus

This appeal to the need of a prior consensus may seem plausible, especially at a time of anxiety about the future and rising conservatism, but it is finally unconvincing. Quite apart from the difficulty of determining what would constitute a *con*sensus in a society made up of more or less *dis*parate groups, there is the problem of justifying the imposition of the caution of the majority on the adventurousness of a minority.[4] It is hard to see why all human beings should be expected to avoid taking risks to the extent required by Dr Harman when in his Dissenting Statement he writes: 'the very fact that we cannot exclude higher than normal risks deriving from the trauma of discovering that an IVF production was compounded with donor sperm and/or donor ovum intervention should make us want to protect the child-adolescent-adult and the community of his/her day from that possibility' (paragraph 8). If all our forebears had adopted that attitude human civilisation would not have made much progress and if Dr Harman were really serious in adopting it, he should demand that all prospective parents undergo genetic screening and that any identified as carriers of abnormalities be prevented from becoming parents.

A principle of justice

The common good and consensus are not the only principles whose collectivist assumptions make them unsuitable for application to a plural society. A unitary conception of social justice suffers from the same defect. This becomes apparent upon examination of the view of fairness taken by the Rev. Dr S. Marshall, SVD, in the submission he made to the Victorian committee following the report on donor gametes. Dr Marshall suggests that when 'medical resources are limited, fairness demands that priority be given to the greatest number of people with the greatest need' and he goes on to express concern at the possibility of the approval given by the committee to IVF being mistaken for a 'justification for allocating more funds to IVF than it warrants'. While it is quite clear from these statements where Dr Marshall's sympathies lie, it is not so clear what he means by giving 'priority' to the greatest number with the greatest need. Since he later bemoans the failure fully to fund such facilities as the Royal Dental Hospital of Melbourne and the Essendon Hospital, it seems likely that he is referring, not to a group to be discovered by a complex formula relating numerical size to gravity of need, but simply to the broad range of those with general medical needs in Victoria. That said, however, it is not at all clear why, at any particular point in time, this or any other group in Victoria should be given 'priority' for the purposes of funding. There are two very important reasons for this lack of clarity. First, the concept of need cannot be neatly formulated and this makes it impossible to rank different kinds of need in an order upon which all may be expected to agree. Granted there may be a measure of agreement about the seriousness of certain needs, it may still be reasonable at a particular time and place to give priority to the treatment of needs on the grounds of their incidence or of their gravity or of their amenability to treatment or of their novelty (to 'nip them in the bud') or of the urgency with which they require treatment or a combination of these and other factors.

Secondly, issues of fairness are too complex to be decided by reference to a single criterion such as need. Attention must also be given to such matters as what people are entitled to expect, what they deserve and what provision is to be made for future generations. It would not be fair to a great many couples who have been placed on the waiting lists for IVF treatment for the resources available to be suddenly and drastically reduced. Futhermore, as I have argued elsewhere concerning the allocation of medical resources, the pioneers of new forms of treatment 'deserve the encouragement to implement new programs and a fair opportunity to prove their worth', especially in view of the possibility that this will bring 'future benefit' to people.[5]

The complexity of the issue of fairness, together with the problem of sorting out which needs are to be served, shows Dr Marshall's submission to be quite simplistic. Priority in the allocation of scarce resources need not always be given to the same group and, indeed, in a plural society it cannot because there is no principle able to command the common commitment that would render such a policy acceptable to all social groups. To claim the contrary is to mask the fact that, in a plural society, one's claim is sectional. Thus the claim that Dr Marshall makes on behalf of the greatest number with the greatest need becomes, as he is honest enough to admit, a claim that he makes on behalf of one hospital because he is a dentist and on behalf of another because he is a nearby resident!

The principle of utility

Numerous submissions made to the Victorian committee reveal that those who are most enthusiastic about the development of IVF are also inclined to use a collectivist principle in order to justify it. The principle is the utilitarian one of judging actions according to their consequences for human happiness. In the case of IVF it is with some plausibility argued that so much happiness will be brought to human lives by its successful employment that only the mean spirited could call it in question. As every critic of utilitarianism knows, however, this kind of argument begs some rather important questions about the price that some people may have to pay for the sake of the fortunate group. Questions have been raised, for example, about the future well-being and, therefore, happiness of the children born as a result of IVF and, while these questions may be more serious in cases where donor gametes are employed, they do serve to remind us that the product of IVF is not just a means to the happiness of others, notably the parents. Less speculative are the questions to be raised about those infertile couples whom IVF locks more firmly into a desperate quest for pregnancy and those who, having failed to achieve this, will feel a heightened sense of isolation and grief. How are the varying effects of IVF to be measured and weighed in the balance? Only by pretending that the different members of society are like the different parts of one body whose head is able to decide which shall be sacrificed so that others may prosper. A plural society, however, is no corporation, still less an organism.

The liberal principle

Confronted with the collectivist implications of the principles according to which many would determine social policy, it is tempting to opt instead for the liberal alternative. This, of course, sets great store by individual freedom of choice and welcomes any development, such as IVF, which expands it. The main point of submissions made by those of a liberal outlook to the Victorian committee, however, has been to oppose any legislative or other restrictions being placed on IVF programs by the State on the grounds that the programs are not causing harm to anybody and that people who object to IVF and related procedures are not obliged to take part in them.[6] Submissions along these lines tend to overlook the same kinds of question as do utilitarian supporters of IVF. In the case of the liberal this reflects a rather atomistic individualism which conceives of harm in terms of the more immediate and discernible effects of the acts of discrete agents and regards longer term and more diffuse societal repercussions as accidental. This explains, but hardly justifies, the impatience of the liberal when some groups express concern about the possible impact that technological intervention will have on attitudes to human sexuality and reproduction or that widespread use of donor gametes will have on the sense of personal identity or confidence in public records. These are matters of some moment and while concern about them may not warrant a total ban being placed on IVF and donor programs, it does suggest that they only be permitted to proceed with caution. Sir Gustav Nossal may be right in saying that the genie is now out of the bottle but this does not mean that (s)he should be permitted to roar around like a lion, devouring whom (s)he will!

The principle of human rights

A development within the liberal tradition that has become particularly influential in contemporary discussion of social issues has been the notion of human rights. Needless to say, the Victorian committee has received submissions championing the rights of one party or another from a variety of sources. Some of these have appealed to the U.N. Declaration on Human Rights and argued that its reference to parenthood means that couples have a right to avail themselves of IVF. This argument rests on a confusion between what has been called a liberty, or an action, right and what has been called a claim, or a recipient, right. In other words, to assert that people have a right to act unimpeded in a certain way is not to suggest that they have a right to claim and receive assistance in so acting. The other party whose rights are vigorously promoted in submissions received by the committee is of course the embryo. Its supposed right to life forms the basis of an argument that it also has a right to be treated with due respect and not to be frozen, experimented upon or casually discarded. Since the IVF programs could not have begun and could not continue without some of these things happening, it is argued that they must be brought to a complete halt. Now, without going into the vexed question of the moral status of an embryo, it can be pointed out that this line of argument, like most which take human rights as their starting point, suffers from the basic flaw that has already been attributed to liberalism, namely individualism. It is assumed that a right is an inalienable possession of an individual and hence, once one is established, that there can be no room for further debate about what moral or social policy should be (unless, of course, the one right comes into conflict with another in a particular set of circumstances). One pair of authors has rather felicitously described this as 'the idea of rights as trumps'. They go on to suggest that rights should not be regarded as the property of discrete individuals but as an indication of what it means to be a person in a particular society. Rights thus have both an individual and a social aspect

and appeals to them serve to indicate that matters of moral importance to both individuals and society are to be debated, not that debate has been brought to an end—'trumped'—by the assertion of a
matter in which the individual invariably has priority over society.[7]

Be all this as it may, it should be clear that liberal principles of
freedom of choice and human rights go too far in seeking to redress
the imbalance of collectivist principles. Indeed, begging as they do
important questions about the social nature of the human person,
they go so far as to close the circle and bring us back to the point
from which we started, where the preference of one social group,
which in the case of the liberal is that with the power to effect its
choice or make good its supposed right, is imposed upon the remainder that make up the plurality. In view of this anomalous situation it seems to me appropriate to follow the course taken by the
Victorian committee in its consideration of the use of donor gametes
in IVF. I would summarise this as an attempt to accommodate as
many as possible of the interests of the parties affected. This amounts
to a procedure for making recommendations concerning public policy, not to a principle or set of principles on which to base such
recommendations.

A procedure for accommodating interests
The Issues Paper that the committee published on *Donor gametes in
IVF* may be interpreted as a preliminary account of the ways in which
it considered the interests of different persons and groups likely to be
affected by the use of donor sperm and ova in order to achieve
pregnancy and the birth of children. In the light of the responses it
received to the Issues Paper, the committee proceeded to form as
common a mind as it could on the matters it had raised and thus to
draft the report, with recommendations, that it subsequently presented to the State Attorney-General. Among the important matters
that were only decided at this late stage were the extent to which
recommendations similar to those concerning the use of donor sperm
could be made about the use of donor ova and embryos and the
amount of information it would be appropriate to exchange between
donors, couples and children.

It has been pointed out that the concept of an interest is more
'fuzzy' and less strong but more subtle than that of a right.[8] This
makes it more possible for a variety of interests to be accommodated
by a particular social policy and this has been the aim of the majority
of the committee in making its recommendations. It certainly did not
take the view expressed by Dr Harman in his Dissenting Statement
that 'the interests of the child are paramount' (paragraph 8), although

it is fair to say that these interests did receive special attention from the committee because it was felt that they have often been over-looked by those concerned about the interests of the medical teams, infertile couples, donors and others. To make one set of interests 'paramount', however, would be to take yet another step in the direction of imposing the needs of one group or the views of another upon the remainder of the plurality and I think that the State of Victoria should be grateful to the committee for refusing to take such a step at this or at other points. For a plural society, lacking as it does a common centre of loyalty, can only remain a desirable context in which to live if the different groups that comprise it are satisfied that, wherever appropriate, their interests are consulted and, wherever possible, they are accommodated.

The human factor

It would be wrong of me to give the impression that the deliberations of the committee have proceeded smoothly along a path that it had mapped out well in advance. In the formulation of social policy, as in every area of life, accidents do happen and they can work in your favour or against you. I think that, as far as the production of its *Report on donor gametes* is concerned, the committee enjoyed a deal of good fortune. Following its Interim Report it had thought of considering such matters as the freezing of embryos before those related to the use of donor gametes but it was diverted from this path by what may be regarded as an accident of history, namely the strong reaction to its Interim Report by couples requiring donor gametes in order to establish a pregnancy and the publicity given to their cause by sections of the media. If the committee had given prior consideration to the handling of embryos it would almost certainly have had to grapple with the issue of the moral status of the embryo and how this would have affected its deliberations concerning the use of donor gametes one can only speculate. It certainly would not have made the task any easier.

The religious factor

If the accidents of history serve as a reminder of human limitations, so too, I believe, do the terms of Christian faith. In particular, I would suggest that hope for the kingdom of God not only provides an incentive to seek change for the better in human society but also carries with it the realisation that all human achievements, of both mind and body, are provisional. This seems to me to go together well with the kind of cautious approval that the Victorian committee has recommended the State give to the development of IVF because it is a form of approval that would serve a variety of human interests while refraining from sitting in final judgment on matters which remain contentious. A certain modesty in contributing to the formulation of social policy should surely characterise those who know that now they see through a glass darkly.

1   *Report on donor gametes in IVF* (hereafter RDG), paragraph 2.6.

2   In making such a statement Dr Harman shows himself to be arguing in terms derived from the moral theological tradition of his church, despite the disclaimer in the opening paragraph of his Dissenting Statement. I should add that he does so in terms which are admirably lucid and that this has been a feature of all his contributions to the work of the committee.

3   The address 'Evil in man—legal considerations' given by Mr Justice F. Brennan to the Fourth Australian Asian–Pacific Forensic Sciences Congress in Sydney near the end of August 1982 gave voice to the argument that scientists and others are mistaken in looking 'to the law to provide guidelines for the application of new reproductive technology beyond the point of a moral consensus'.

4   I do not say that this is impossible, as is the case with the common good.

5   'IVF and the human family' in William Walters & Peter Singer (eds), *Test-tube babies,* Oxford University Press, Melbourne, 1982, p. 83.

6   The latter is an argument that the committee itself has employed; see RDG 2.6.

7   Larry R. Churchill & José Jorge Simán, 'Abortion and the rhetoric of individual rights', *The Hastings Center Report,* vol. 12, no. 1, February 1982, pp. 9–12.

8   J. R. Lucas, *On justice,* Clarendon, Oxford, 1980, ch. 2, esp. pp. 24 f.

4

Anglicanism, ethics, moral theology and contrived conception

John Morgan

The Anglican Church has never possessed a fully developed and systematic moral theology. This has served as both curse and blessing. On the one hand, it has meant that the Anglican Church has had relatively few strictly defined and detailed moral teachings, and thus difficulties are experienced by individual Anglicans when moral decisions have to be made at a particular level. On the other hand, it has meant that, when the need has arisen to make any statement, the Church or its representative bodies are able to be responsive to contemporary issues, without necessarily being shackled by theologically outmoded assumptions.[1]

The generalisation that Anglican laity make moral decisions without firm ecclesiastical statements to guide them is, however, not without some individual exceptions. On the question of the use of contraception within marriage, for example, the Lambeth Conferences of Anglican bishops from all over the world made clear statements condemning contraception at both the 1908 and 1920 Conferences. Ironically, Anglican people, having been given authoritative and unambiguous advice by their hierarchy, chose to ignore it. The 1930 Lambeth Conference shifted its stance partly as the result of the fact that a moral judgment had already been formed amongst the laity that the use of contraception within marriage was morally valid. The bishops at this Conference also took into account changed insights into the nature of marriage, population pressure in some countries, and the changing status of women.

When the Anglican Church in its various national manifestations, or one of its agencies, such as the Board for Social Responsibility in England or the Australian Social Responsibilities Commission, attempts to make a judgment on the moral licitness of any scientific advance or social practice, they are usually eclectic in approach. This is partly brought about by the diffuse membership of the Church in the U.K. and Australia, which keeps it fairly closely tied to the general morality of the community.

A further reason for Anglican eclecticism is that it is heir to both catholic and protestant theological traditions, and for that reason is not tied to any single methodology when it approaches a moral question. The *via media* which characterises Anglicanism involves consideration of Scripture, tradition and the insights of human reason. The more catholic-minded Anglicans will emphasise the authority and teaching role of the Church interpreted by reason, while those who incline to the reformed outlook will perhaps give greater weight to Scripture and individual judgment.

Harmon Smith has suggested that modern Anglican moral theology finds itself faced not with just its catholic tradition and reformed perspective, but it must now also come to terms with the autonomous reason of the modern scientific outlook in the light of the first two. Like all value-bearing institutions in contemporary society, the Anglican Church must face in addition the effect of the loss of any authoritative tradition and still seek—as it does in its liturgy—to incorporate human life into divine grace.[2]

It is all too easy in the present to separate the realms of nature and grace. At a practical level, Anglicanism, by virtue of its incarnational emphasis in theology, has always regarded human activities as worthwhile, and tended to look at any judgment of them in a developmental manner. Austin Farrer expressed this when he wrote:

> Practical (moral) judgment does not proceed from facts to inferred probability, nor from an addition of probabilities to a firmer probability. It proceeds from suasion to persuasion, from tentative to final response.[3]

Thus, when the Social Responsibilities Commission of the Anglican Church in Australia considered the question of the ethics of in vitro fertilisation, it found it had no specific teaching in this area and no single approach. It is certainly true that there were teachings (of a definitive type) available in related areas, such as those on abortion, given by various Lambeth Conferences of the Anglican bishops, and there were certainly various viewpoints based on natural law tradition, as from some theologians within the Roman Catholic Church, as well as various papal teachings. Pope Pius XII, for example, had condemned the whole technique in a statement made when he addressed the Second World Congress on Fertility and Sterility (1956). He said that 'attempts at artificial human fecundation *in vitro* . . . must be rejected as immoral and absolutely unlawful'.

The formulation of an Australian Anglican viewpoint

The Australian Anglican SRC represents the whole spectrum of Anglicanism. The Commission had not made many statements relating to the biomedical sciences prior to the advent of IVF in Australia. The first statement in this area, which was made in December 1981, expressed the concern of many people in the general community over what was seen as insufficient debate regarding the ethics of various aspects of attempts to secure pregnancy outside normal marital coitus. In issuing the statement, the Commission recognised the tensions and ambiguity which so often exist within many human activities:

> Christians are given two factors which exist in tension. One is our belief in the supremacy of a sovereign God. He is a God who creates and sustains life. To fulfil this purpose he often uses human co-operation. The second factor in the tension is the human propensity for evil. The potential for evil in this biotechnology is great. Current experimentation demands careful debates and public accountability.[5]

This statement represents much that is characteristic of the Anglican approach. For example, Reinhold Niebuhr once remarked during the 1930s that Anglicans were Christians with an Augustinian (sin-laden) prayer book, while, on the other hand, the preaching of Anglican clergy was largely Pelagian, exhorting good people to be better or seeking to point basically good people in the right direction.

Early in 1982 the particular case of IVF was considered by the SRC. The Commission found itself divided between those who espoused a particular form of natural law viewpoint and those who emphasised the role of human co-creativity as a divine gift to be exercised responsibly.

The Commission, like the Secretary of the Church of England Board for Social Responsibility when IVF first became a practical possibility, gave a cautious endorsement to the use of IVF within an infertile marriage. Guidelines were also advanced for the operation of the process and further questions were asked about the control of it. This attempt to inform the public debate, and to ensure that full ethical guidelines were established, is also in line with much that has characterised the modern Anglican approach to moral problems—to deal with specifics, and at the same time to look at the questions concerning the broad public good. Some of this approach reveals the legacy of Anglicanism as being concerned with the whole of society rather than simply with the practices of the faithful alone. It must be noted, however, that many natural law approaches to moral problems seek to address society at large, including both believers and non-believers.

In evidence presented (by the SRC) to the Victorian government committee of inquiry on IVF (the Waller committee), some aspects of the majority viewpoint were spelt out. The provisional nature of moral teaching in this area was noted, and it was acknowledged that the newness of some of the techniques meant that a careful evaluation had yet to be made. Hard questions do not yield easy and immediate answers. IVF was seen to stand in need of justification. The fact that some cases of female infertility could be overcome by IVF was seen as a legitimate form of therapy and consistent with the Christian understanding of the medical role. Further, the process also led to the birth of a child and the building up of a family. Both the therapeutic and family aspects were seen as legitimate human 'goods' which could be given theological justification. Thus, the disvalue of separating human fertilisation from the act of love making was seen to be overcome by the realisation of these morally good ends. This was not, of course, the same thing as saying that one was simply doing evil in order to achieve good.

The approach which underlies this viewpoint is that of proportionate reason—the *ratio proportionata*—an ethical approach which, though of quite ancient lineage, has recently come to the forefront of discussion in modern Roman Catholic moral theology.[6] According to this view, the employment of IVF within marriage would not be using an evil or a wrong means to overcome another evil. One is bringing a child into being, by use of a God-given technology derived from the gifts which God has given humanity in order to further God-given ends. The proportionate reason argument contradicts any view which would reject IVF on the grounds of a wrong relationship between object, ends and circumstances.

This is not an embracing of a utilitarian or teleological approach to ethics; rather it is an approach which has elements of both deontological and teleological systems. An end—the birth of a child—is sought. This is an ethical good. Since it brings a new human life into being, and it assists the parents whose marriage and personal relationship is completed, it is seen to be in accord with God's plan for humanity.

The means are not ideal, since pain, discomfort and expense are involved. For some theological writers, that which should not be separated is deliberately separated. But, of course, it cannot be otherwise.[7] Why then should it be labelled as immoral or unethical? The critics answer that the use of such technology undermines a God-given nexus, and hence they imply that if a couple is childless and this can only be overcome by IVF, then they should remain childless. Such a view is deeply suspicious of all human achievements in the area of science; indeed it is suspicious of human nature itself.

But to refer again to the notion of proportionate reason. Part of the use of it involves the way in which one seeks the ethical good that is pursued.[8] No one believes that it is good in itself to separate coitus and fertilisation, but we need to ask if by doing this, as in IVF, we will do violence to the very things which we are attempting to build up by normal procreation, and which the act of marital coitus facilitates, i.e. human family life. According to those critics who believe that they base their case on natural law, the act of IVF is intrinsically evil. But looked at in the light of intention, process/act and consequences, the proportionalist will conclude that it is a morally good act. It is not concentration on the end alone that makes the action of IVF good; it is that the act within an infertile marriage is not wrong, and indeed may be regarded as right and good in the total context of the divine order. This approach obviously involves elements of teleology and deontology, as well, of course, as a scriptural view or valuation of marriage and family life as given by God and approved of by Jesus.

With regard to the concept of natural law, Anglican moral theology and ethics does indeed employ it, but not necessarily in the sense claimed by some of its supposed adherents. The moral life, according to natural law theory in the widest sense, relates to wholeness and the fulfilment of human nature. The act of building up a family would thus be entirely in accord with this understanding of natural law. For example, the modern Anglican writer David Brown denies that natural law has anything to do with law in the sense of highly specific injunctions to action, or with nature in the widest sense. He claims that it is 'based on the view that human nature has been so fashioned by God that it is only by leading a moral life that certain basic demands of its nature can be satisfied'; thus the moral imperatives stem from the basic demands of human nature.[9] On this view of natural law, the action of IVF would be both entirely good and right when one could not build up a family in any other way. This kind of use of natural law is based on revelation and doctrine, rather than simply on observation of nature itself. Thus we can see a misconstrual of the Christian idea of natural law, by regarding it as naturalistic positivism, in the remarks of two authors who, bent on criticising IVF, lump it together with artificial insemination by donor, and claim that what we have in both is 'an unnecessary attack on nature involving the destruction of human persons and the violation of the ethical integrity of natural marriage'.[10]

The status of the early embryo

Some authors assert that IVF is unacceptable to those who would hold to the Judaeo-Christian interpretation of the value of human life. The Anglican SRC demonstrated its concern for human life by calling on those scientists engaged in IVF to try to limit the loss of early embryonic life in the process. However, the Commission recognised that some embryo loss would occur and the concern was that this be kept to a minimum.[11] It was understood too that something like 50 to 60 per cent of all embryos are lost in attempts to procure pregnancy by means of normal coitus. The SRC did not necessarily embrace a fully developmental view of the value of human life. Most Anglicans would recognise, however, that within the history of Christianity the absolutist opinion which regards the embryo as inviolable from the moment of conception is, in fact, a relatively recent view, i.e. they would incline to the view that humanity develops along with embryonic and foetal development, but this is a probable opinion.

Human life is, in the Judaeo-Christian tradition, seen as a great gift from God and to be valued above any other natural thing. Therefore respect for human life is called for at all stages, but not at a purely physical level alone. The SRC does not believe that experimental work should be performed on early embryos deliberately produced for that purpose. On the other hand, the freezing of excess embryos produced by the IVF programs in order to preserve them for later replacement was not altogether ruled out, since it was requested in a subsequent statement that such freezing should be kept to a minimum. This was in order to preserve the witness to the value of human life, without necessarily making a judgment that human life in the fullest sense is present from the moment of conception.[12]

The problem posed here is whether we abrogate a fundamental moral principle by any action which involves intervention with early embryos. There is no doubt that we need to protect human life, and especially early human life, in a world where thousands of foetuses are aborted each year. However, we might well ask whether in all circumstances we should prohibit any or all research involving embryos up to the end of the pre-implantation stages of growth.

Such work with early embryos might well enable us to analyse genes in the cells of these early embryos so that genetically transferred defects might be repaired. This could significantly reduce the present tendency to simply abort defective foetuses. Such abortions often occur late in pregnancy with traumatic effects on women and, of course, with loss of life by the foetus. Gene therapy might well become possible as the result of experimental work on early embryos to the foetal stage.

Dr John Fletcher (not to be confused with Joseph Fletcher), an Anglican ethicist working as an adviser at the National Institutes of Health in the U.S.A., has made a strong case for the observation of, and limited experimentation with, early embryos in his work *Coping with genetic disorders*. This book combines a principled ethical approach and deep pastoral sensitivity with a full understanding of the scientific processes. He believes that gene therapy should be tried, first, with high-risk genetic disorders, like Lesch-Nyhan syndrome. No treatment is available at present for this condition, which afflicts only males, normally killing them off in their teens. It is characterised by high concentrations of uric acid in the blood, abnormal movements of the body, mental retardation, and involuntary biting of the lips and fingers. John Fletcher says of research in this area:

> The goal of human genetics should be primarily the search for better understanding of the ways and means to emancipate human beings from the burden of suffering brought on by random changes in the genes. A mutant gene for Lesch-Nyhan disease or sickle cell disease is a form of bondage. These mutants are threats that more evil than good will exist for the affected persons. We need to be cautious about research in genetics, but we must not, in my view, neglect to do the great good that can be done if the scientific possibilities allow for it.

For Fletcher the conclusions of his religious faith are that some risk taking is justified in the scientific area, and that specifically, in this area, it could, by the alleviation of the burden of suffering, be a means of demonstrating the goodness of God and the meaning of participation in God's emancipating work.

This approach is not altogether unlike where it seems that Bernard Häring's logic is leading him when he talks about genetic experimentation for the sake of human self-improvement as being morally permissible.[14]

In a number of papers Professor Gordon Dunstan, the leading modern Anglican moral theologian working in the area of medical ethics, has recently questioned the absolute prohibition of work on pre-implantation stage embryos. He bases his case, in part, on a developmental view of the humanity of the embryo and sees this as compatible with a deep respect for human life. Professor Dunstan says that, historically, the tradition (relating to the value of foetal life) attempted to grade the protection accorded to the nascent human according to the stages of its development, and a particular view of ensoulment. While he sees the absolutist viewpoint as valuable, in the face of the erosion of human life, we run, he believes, the danger of losing great benefits to humanity. 'But we have to choose', he writes.

> Uterine life must be accorded protection at some point. If we put that point too early, forbidding observation and experimental use of pre-implantation embryos in the early stages of cell division, we shall inhibit much useful research of potential human benefit, including the improvement of the chances of successful pregnancy for lack of which many extra embryos are sacrificed at present. Embryologists themselves search for means of determining a point beyond which experiment would be intolerable; they would relate that point to the beginning of the development of the nervous system, anticipating the capacity of the foetus for sensitivity or awareness—words used by Dante, as we have seen, as characteristic of the foetus so grown as to warrant the attribution of rational human soul. Knowledge in embryology may change; but perhaps there are aspects of human relating to it which are perennial.[15]

Dunstan's approach relates benefits to principles and seeks also to relate the status of the embryo to both scientific and theological understandings by questioning the claim that life begins at the moment of conception. This is a lively area of discussion amongst theologians at present. It is said that Karl Rahner, for example, has reached different conclusions from those expressed in Pope John Paul II's 1982 statement which condemned 'experimental manipulations of the human embryo, since the human being, from conception to death, cannot be exploited for any purpose whatsoever'.[16] The Social Responsibilities Commission of the Anglican Church of Australia stands opposed to uninhibited research involving human embryos and has requested that human embryos should be treated with the utmost respect.[17] Whether this means that all research involving human embryos should be forbidden must await further discussion.

Regardless of what line of theological reasoning is adopted in looking at the questions raised by developments in the biomedical sciences, there is wide and substantial agreement on the need to protect the distinctively human and the value of life. This agreement does not always lead necessarily to the same conclusions, since different methods are used to address the questions. All within the Anglican Church would agree that we should not necessarily do all that we seem to be able to do. Technology and the research which underlies it bring great benefits to humanity, but there are times when the cost seems too great. This was well put at both the scientific and ethical levels by Lewis Thomas, a perceptive medical scientist, when he wrote that: 'Every important scientific advance that has come in looking like an answer has turned, sooner or later—usually sooner—into a question. And the game is just beginning'.[18]

1   J. L. Morgan, A sociological analysis of some developments in the moral theology of the Church of England since 1900, D.Phil. thesis, Oxford University, 1976, pp. 429–33.

2   H. L. Smith, 'Contraception and natural law: a half-century of Anglican moral reflection', in Paul Elmen (ed.), *The Anglican moral choice,* Wilton, Connecticut, 1983, pp. 199–200.

3   A. Farrer, *Finite and infinite,* Westminster, 1943, p. 145.

4   Quoted in Leroy Walters, 'Human in vitro fertilization: a review of the ethical literature', *The Hastings Center Report,* vol. 9, no. 4, August 1979, p. 25.

5   Social Responsibilities Commission press release, 2 December 1981. The statement was attributed to the Bishop of Bendigo, the Rt Rev. O. S. Heyward.

6   See the discussion in Richard McCormick & Paul Ramsey (eds), *Doing evil to achieve good,* Chicago, 1978, esp. pp. 29–34.

7   Note also the distinction between moral evil and intrinsic evil in the discussion by Richard McCormick in Notes on moral theology: 1982, *Theological Studies,* vol. 44, no. 1, March 1983, and the discussion also by McCormick of the right reason *(recto ratio)* as related to the use of proportionate reason *(ratio proportionata)* in Notes on moral theology: 1981, *Theological Studies,* vol. 43, no. 1, March 1982, pp. 69–92.

8   A possible approach to this from a pluralistic deontological viewpoint could be based on W. D. Ross's distinction between actual duties and prima facie duties. Ross used the latter to distinguish between duties binding on all occasions unless they are in conflict with stronger duties. One's actual moral duty in a situation is determined by an examination of all the competing prima facie duties. Intuition is used to discover the principles, but one must decide by perception (à la Aristotle) the greatest balance of right over wrong. See the discussion in Tom L. Beauchamp & James F. Childress, *Principles of biomedical ethics,* New York, 1979, p. 35.

9   David Brown, *Choices: ethics and the Christian,* Oxford, 1983, p. 81. Brown's understanding is similar to that of another Anglican writer, Keith Ward. In *The divine image,* London, 1976, p. 101, Ward says of natural law: '. . . this is *not* a naturalistic theory—a theory which founds

morality simply on facts about human nature, or which asserts that nature's purposes, whatever they are, should not be impeded. For the very conception of human nature on which it builds is the notion of an ideal nature, the *imago Dei,* which is commanded by God, and in accordance with which actual nature must be shaped by man's free action; so it is explicityly non-naturalistic'.

10   Daniel Ch. Overduin & John I. Fleming, *Life in a test-tube,* Adelaide, 1982, p. 222.

11   Submission to the Waller committee, 1982.

12   Social Responsibilities Commission press release, 'Limit called to embryo freezing'.

13   John C. Fletcher, *Coping with genetic disorders: a guide for clergy and parents,* San Francisco, 1982, p. 174.

14   Bernard Häring, *Free and faithful in Christ: moral theology for priests and laity,* vol. 3, pp. 26–7. Cf. the remarks of Clive Cookson, science correspondent for *The Times* (London), 21 December 1983, p. 5. 'Many people react strongly against the idea of tampering with the genetic make-up of humanity as it has evolved. Few, however, could object to "phenotypic" therapy with the aim of curing a disease by changing the genes, in, for example, blood cells, for the life-time of an individual'.

15   Gordon Dunstan, The moral status of the early embryo: a tradition recalled, unpublished paper, 1983, p. 14. This has been presented as evidence to the U.K. Department of Health and Social Security Inquiry into IVF, AID and related issues (the Warnock Committee).

16   q.v. Richard McCormick, Notes on moral theology: 1982, op. cit, p. 122.

17   The National Health and Medical Research Council Medical Research Ethics Committee, in its report on *Ethics in medical research involving the human fetus and human fetal tissue,* October 1983, has said that continuation of embryonic development in vitro beyond the stage at which implantation would normally occur is not acceptable (p. 36).

18   Lewis Thomas, *Late night thoughts on listening to Mahler's Ninth Symphony,* New York, 1983, p. 155.

5

IVF from a biblical perspective

Michael Hill

In vitro fertilisation (IVF) is a procedure which allows an ovum to be fertilised, and grown for a short time, outside the womb in a dish. The basic question before us is whether or not it is ethical to subject human gametes to this procedure. The procedure opens up a number of other technical possibilities such as sperm and ova donation and the use of surrogate wombs. With these possibilities come further ethical questions. If we take the authority of the Bible seriously, how are we to attempt to answer such questions?

Clearly the biblical writers did not envisage such procedures and they provide us with no moral injunctions one way or the other. Nevertheless while the Bible has nothing directly to say on these matters we are not justified in concluding that the Bible is irrelevant in regard to these issues. Most Christian writers on these subjects do not seem to think that the Bible is irrelevant. They argue that the procedures either conflict or do not conflict with certain values or principles found in Scripture. For example, many argue that the IVF procedure itself conflicts with the principle of the sanctity of life.

The validity of this type of approach needs to be challenged. Being *ad hoc* in nature it can and does lead to dilemmas which the method itself is not capable of resolving. For example, some might want to argue that since God commands mankind to be fruitful and multiply (Genesis 1:28) IVF is a helpful and moral procedure. On the other hand, others argue that since IVF involves the disposal of fertilised

47

ova it contradicts the principle of the sanctity of life (Genesis 9:6). An *ad hoc* method provides no way of choosing between these two principles.

What is required if we are going to make truly *biblical* moral judgments is a unified and integrated biblical theology where the parts (including the moral principles and values) are placed within the context of the whole. Disregard for the theological movement and structures of Scripture will inevitably lead to the misapplication of moral principles. These misapplications well might fly in the face of the overall thrust of the Scriptures.

Locating a unified and integrated biblical theology is an ongoing and never-ending task. As we read the parts of the Bible and come to an understanding of the whole so our understanding of the whole provides a new framework and context for a better understanding of the parts. Refinement of our understanding will always be possible in this life. (That we only know in part is true in more ways than one.) Some people will have a more integrated understanding than others. For our purposes it will be enough to recognise that the Bible presents us with what is essentially one story. It begins with creation and ends with the new creation. In between creation and the new creation we find the Fall, covenant(s) which regulate(s) the consequent broken relationships, and the Christ event which restores and heals broken relationships.

Before we can proceed to make any moral judgments we need to decide upon a theory of moral obligation. The need for a theory of moral obligation can best be explained by giving an example. Utilitarians have a theory of obligation. It is an instrument which helps them rationally determine their moral obligations. In crude terms the theory states that they are to do that which brings about the greatest balance of good over harm to the greatest number of people. Utilitarians differ over what they consider the good to be. Some hold that there are many goods while others hold that there is just one. Hedonistic utilitarians hold that there is only one thing which is of value and that is pleasure. Let us suppose that we are hedonistic utilitarians and believe that pleasure is the good and pain is evil. We would have a rational mechanism for working out what we *ought* to do. Any action or rule which brings about the greatest amount of pleasure for the greatest number of people becomes obligatory. On the other hand we would be obligated *not* to do any action or follow any rule which brought about a balance of pain over pleasure. Given the normal circumstances of life truth telling, for example, becomes obligatory on this theory. Similarly we would be obligated not to do those things that cause pain, be it mental or physical.

Obviously none of the biblical writers were concerned to develop a theory of obligation, yet there is one buried in the biblical material for it is full of injunctions about people's obligations. Debate continues over whether the biblical ethic is teleological or deontological. All the theories of obligation, such as the utilitarian theory outlined above, which calculate the rightness or wrongness of any action or rule in terms of the non-moral consequences (such as pleasure) are called teleological theories. Theories which deny that the non-moral consequences are the sole factor in determining obligations are called deontological theories.

My own opinion is that it can be stated either way but that the teleological version is much more capable of use in relation to contemporary issues not envisaged in the Scriptures. The very nature of Scripture, because it is concerned with the purposes of God in creation, lends itself to a teleological statement.

Clearly God's purpose is to establish a community. Relationships within this community are to reflect the relationships within the Godhead. The complement of male and female (that is, mankind) is made in the image of God (Genesis 1:27). God's community or kingdom is to be bonded together by love. The bonding is to have both a vertical and horizontal direction. Jesus effectively summarised all of his Father's instruction to his people in terms of love (Matthew 22:37–40).

It does not appear unjustified to propose as an ultimate principle in a biblical theory of obligation something along the following lines. *Always do that which generates or maintains love relationships with God and man.* (As a love relationship with God necessarily involves a love relationship with one's fellows we could just state the principle in terms of a love relationship with God. But this might mean losing sight of a necessary element.)

On this principle it would become obligatory to do that which would generate love relationships. Loving your neighbour would become obligatory since your love may evoke a loving response and this would generate a love relationship. Likewise it would become obligatory not to do those things such as coveting and lying which break love relationships.

The word 'love' refers to the biblical concept and not the many ambiguous contemporary concepts. For this reason I would like to replace the word 'love' by the word *agape*. In the Bible the word *agape* refers to an act of the will which determines to do nothing but good, where there is opportunity, to those to whom it is directed. It is an act of will which brings about a benevolent attitude. Agape towards another person will be expressed in terms of meeting that person's proper needs and desires, be they biological, psychological or whatever. Agape towards God can only be expressed in terms of obedience. In a perfect or unfallen world love towards our neighbour would also be expressed by obedience (or, at least, submission to our neighbour's requests).

Our ultimate principle declares that the thing of ultimate value is not agape but agape relationships. Agape is an act of will and a consequent attitude. Any one person can have an attitude of love. But an agape relationship requires two persons bonded by agape towards each other. Basically an agape relationship is a psychological state—its essence is commitment of both parties to each other.

Agape and, therefore, agape relationships require knowledge. To will and to do good for someone requires a knowledge of the nature of that person. Fortunately there seems to be an essential nature common to all mankind which makes the acquisition of this knowledge a less arduous task than it might have been if everybody was completely unique.

Agape relationships cross genetic boundaries. In the Scriptures agape is not confined to kin. Yet within the Old Testament the social unit for agape relationships is the family. Pragmatically it is not possible to have agape relationships with everyone. Right from the beginning the family is envisaged as the basic social unit. When Genesis 2:24 declares that a man shall leave his father and mother and cleave to his wife and they shall become one flesh it is explaining and endorsing the normal way of establishing a new social unit. In the Old Testament the word 'flesh' denotes kinship. Anything which threatens this prescribed unit is itself proscribed or forbidden. Adultery is proscribed because it threatens the agape relationship between husband and wife and this agape relationship is the foundation of the family unit. Not just any agape relationship can form the basis of a family unit. Because the image of God is found in the male−female complement then the social unit is established by the male leaving his family and being coupled with his wife to form a new unit. Given the theology of the first few chapters of Genesis it is not surprising that homosexual relations are condemned in several places in Scripture.

The Old Testament material is complicated by the fact that the family as the social unit is the unit of inheritance and the inheritance in the land is a share in God's blessing. To be barren is a curse and all sorts of provisions are made so that the patriarch married to a barren women might have an heir. For example, they could raise up children by their wife's handmaid. Similarly the custom of levirate marriage provided the patriarch who was sterile with the hope that he would be provided with an heir even after he was dead.

All of the laws and customs relating to the provision of an heir could bear detailed study. Having a child by the wife's female slave could be analogous to having a child by in vitro fertilisation with a donated ovum. Likewise having a child by the dead husband's brother or close relative could bear analogy to having a child by IVF with donor sperm. The difficulty in establishing these analogies is found in what must be an important motive behind these laws and customs. The concern was to secure a share in the inheritance of the land—a share in God's blessing. Within the framework of Scripture there is a development of the understanding of God's blessing. There is a movement from the garden of Eden to the promised land and on to heaven (a spiritual realm in the presence of God). While all these images of God's blessing differ, the motif of agape relationships is constant. Sonship and the inheritance is given to all in Christ, not just to the first-born male Jew (Galatians 3:28).

Since the inheritance is spiritualised in the New Testament it might be argued that what counts is the spiritual relationship of love and therefore the Old Testament emphasis on kinship can be abandoned. If so, then the requirement of a genetic relationship between both parents and their children can also be relinquished. Alternatively it could be argued that since the motive for the practices which might generate precedents for us today is missing—we no longer have to secure a share in the inheritance through procreation—then the practices (or analogous practices) are no longer justified. The fact that none of the Old Testament practices break the family bond is significant since the New Testament seems to reinforce the notion of the family as the basic social unit (for example 1 Timothy 3:2 and 5:8).

Leaving aside the question of the donation of gametes for the moment, consideration of the biblical material above leads to fairly substantial conclusions. The assumption underlying the material seems to be that if there is an empirical possibility that a child might be conceived and born then that possibility had to be encompassed and framed within the boundaries of an agape relationship between a man and his wife. Moreover both the husband and wife must intend to establish an agape relationship with the child. That is, they must intend to love the child. Given this material and its underlying assumption then a moral judgment about IVF appears relatively straightforward. *There is no moral objection to the use of the procedure provided it is used to help a loving married couple to have a child of their own.* There would be moral objections to using the procedure with single parents or homosexual couples, or in scientific research where the appropriate framework was missing.

A number of objections to IVF still have to be faced. Perhaps the most pressing is the argument based on the status of the fertilised ovum as a human life. The intentional destruction or disposal of fertilised ova is considered by many to be a form of murder. This objection can be bypassed by using various techniques. Fertilising and implanting only one ovum at a time does not involve the intentional destruction of a fertilised ovum, but it does reduce the probability of success. Alternatively a number of ova can be fertilised and implanted in the womb provided the recipient is happy with the possibility of multiple births. Objections to masturbation can also be bypassed by using another technique for collecting sperm.

While it is not possible to resolve the question of gamete donation in the space of this short chapter it is possible to draw attention to the direction in which the biblical ethic moves. If we contrast the biblical ethic of agape relationships with a modern ethic based on individual self-satisfaction then that direction becomes abundantly clear. If individual self-satisfaction is the ultimate source of meaning and value then one would be justified in carefully selecting the donors of gametes to secure those traits and abilities which would guarantee the greatest amount of self-satisfaction for the individual. The biblical ethic does not lead us in this direction. Rather it suggests that even the person with the humblest of abilities can enjoy agape relationships to the full.

In all our discussion and argument the biblical perspective that children are a very special blessing must not be lost. It is natural that parents who share an agape relationship should want to give the opportunity of agape relationships to others through the generation of children. The generation of children provides a richer and wider field of agape relationships and so enriches life for all involved.

Brief statement on author's position and status

Michael Hill is the rector of a Sydney parish who formerly lectured at Moore Theological College in Philosophy and Ethics. Arguing from the basis of a unified and integrated biblical theology he concludes that there are no moral objections to the use of IVF with married couples where the gametes are not donated. Concerned to provide the basis from which our thinking might begin rather than achieve a resolution of all the issues, he suggests that we construct a theory of moral obligation based on love relationships.

6

A case against IVF based on the moral status of the embryo

John Fleming

Some ethical considerations

For many people 'in vitro fertilisation' (IVF) is a self-authenticating medical procedure. A formerly childless couple are given a pregnancy and, all going well, a healthy newborn baby. Who would object to that?

But if we are to judge the moral acceptability of anything that we do solely by the results achieved, then we are involved in a form of decision making which is subjective and in opposition to the Christian tradition.

Christian ethical reflection is rooted in Holy Scripture and natural law. We always have before us the ideal, that which God requires of us if we are to live according to his will.

At the same time we live in a sinful and fallen world. Through sin and weakness we are not always able to live up to the ideal which faithfulness to the Gospel demands of us. God understands and welcomes us back with compassion, with love and forgiveness.

However, if morality is not objective and is to be assessed only in terms of the 'outcome' of an action, then there are no ideals or moral absolutes, and, in the end, nothing which requires confession and divine forgiveness.

It is the view of this writer that there are God-given moral laws the observance of which is essential if society is to survive and if justice is to be available to all people, regardless of race, religion, class, or how old they happen to be. We are obliged to obey these laws, which are evident both to Christians and to non-Christians. Such an obligation to obedience is typical of deontological ethics, and is predicated upon there being some agreed moral norms by which we are bound.

An example of the natural law and the laws of humanity is the command 'You shall not kill'. In a fallen world we may be faced with a situation in which there is no simple choice to be made. In those hard cases, such as an attack by an unjustified aggressor, force and even killing might be justified. But it is a justification for a regrettable necessity given the sin of humanity.

But generally, given the few hard case exceptions, we believe it wrong to kill another human being even if the results of that person's death may include some other person's happiness. And we feel confident to make that assertion, that killing other people is simply against what any reasonable person would regard as a morally safe thing to do.

The right of a person to live is the most fundamental right. It is not given to us by the state. It is something which is due to us simply by virtue of the fact that we are human. Whenever that fundamental right is ignored or overridden we have gross injustice and often social chaos. The objectivity of this position ought to be obvious. The Nazis were found guilty of 'crimes against humanity' even though what they did was at the lawful command of the state.

There is a higher law—natural law—through which God speaks to us, and to which we have a first loyalty. That is why human rights organisations appeal to the peoples of the world over the heads of governments.

The issues

What has all this to do with IVF? A great deal, since one of the principal objections to IVF is that thousands of human beings are sacrificed each year in the IVF programs around the world in order to achieve a relatively few pregnancies.

The human beings that die are human embryos. These human embryos may be discarded as unworthy to be replaced in the female uterus, used as a means of facilitating a single pregnancy, or seen simply as the object of further scientific research.

The essential question involved is the moral status of the human embryo. If the human embryo is not to be regarded as a human person with a right to life, how is it to be regarded? Who is to decide? What rights, if any, should it have? One notes the refusal of committees, both State and church, to confront this issue and make a clear statement of position. This is not a matter to be decided upon by opinion polls. In previous eras a majority of people accepted the slave trade, with all its economic benefits, based, though it was, on the view that some human beings were of less importance than others.

The second major ethical issue which IVF raises concerns the separation of human procreation from human sexual intercourse. IVF does not 'cure' infertility. It bypasses it. Some people argue that IVF merely completes the sexual union of husband and wife. Others argue that IVF is a laboratory technique that supplants natural sexual intercourse.

Finally, the ethical decisions taken concerning the moral status of the human embryo and the separation of procreation from intercourse will condition the ethical decisions taken concerning experimentation on human embryos (including freezing), the gestation of children outside the uterus, the use of donor gametes, and the provision of IVF children for unmarried couples.

The moral status of the human embryo

The question of the moral status of the embryo is fundamental to a consideration of the ethical rightness or wrongness of IVF. It is a fact that there is an embryo wastage in excess of 90 per cent of the embryos produced.[1] Other studies by Nicholas Tonti-Filippini, Research Officer of the St Vincent's Bioethics Centre, support the same conclusion. IVF programs are reluctant to give too much detail of such a high wastage, but no one denies it.

This means that we have to be clear about the moral status of the beings who are destroyed, washed away, experimented on and otherwise wasted in the IVF program. There is no point in relegating such an issue to the 'too hard' basket and then proceeding to justify IVF for childless couples. This is the line followed by hospital ethics committees and State commissions of inquiry, on which, incidentally, there are Christian priests and ministers.

If the embryo has no right to live as a human being, clearly the destruction of such embryos is not a moral problem for the IVF program. Further there can be no objection to freezing embryos or otherwise experimenting on them. If the embryo has a right to live because it is to be considered equally human with any of us, then there is a serious objection to the IVF program and its related experimental activities.

It is argued by those who believe the human embryo is not to be granted a right to live that the embryo is not a human person. It is agreed that it is a human being, it is alive and contains the full genetic identity that it will have for the rest of its life. But it is not a human person.

Personhood is something which is achieved. After the embryo has developed to a certain stage, when it is capable of performing certain functions, it may be regarded as a person. Until then, it is only a potential person.

What criteria can be used to determine personhood? Different people suggest different criteria. Joseph Fletcher, an American medical ethicist, has constructed a 'profile of man' in concrete and discrete terms. He has a list of fifteen positive and five negative 'human criteria'. The positive criteria include:

intelligence (an individual who falls below the IQ 40 mark is questionable as a person; below the 20 mark, not a person)
self-awareness
self-control
a sense of time
the capability of relating to others
concern for others
communication
control of existence[2]

However, there are some significant difficulties with this 'achievement' model of personhood.

According to Fletcher, anyone who lacks just one of his criteria is not a person and therefore has no right to live. His criterion of IQ would mean that no one was human who was a baby or even a child. Indeed uneducated people in isolated communities would almost certainly fail the IQ test of personhood. Again, babies, particularly newborn, might well fail the tests of self-awareness, self-control, a sense of time and so on. As far as 'control of existence' is concerned, no one has that facility. We exist because of God's gracious goodness.

Second, if we say that personhood is achieved we have to face the fact that personhood can be lost. Someone who becomes handicapped either through disease, accident or simply old age would be at risk. This is a most serious matter. If we wish to justify the wastage of human embryos on the grounds they are not human we are, in fact, driving a wedge between humanity and personhood that will have serious implications for all human beings at any stage of the human life cycle.

Third, nature does not revolve around function. Function revolves around nature. I do certain things because I am human. For example, the gift of language. I speak in the way humans use language to communicate because I am human. I am not human because I can speak. Otherwise a deaf mute would be held to be not human.

I am able to participate in human procreation because I am human. If I were infertile this should not be taken to indicate that I am not human. Again, my ability to control myself in the way human beings control and discipline their lives is because I am human. I must not assume, however, that those disturbed people who cannot control themselves are not human.

The idea that we achieve 'personhood' is based on very subjective criteria which, if generally applied, would question the rights of a good many people to exist. Further the word person is left undefined. Sometimes the word is used simply to mean a human being while at other times it is used to refer to personal characteristics.

In the ethical sense, person refers to moral status and when we are to regard a human being as having rights. Some people have suggested that apart from Fletcher's criteria the embryo does not look like a person and is in fact only a potential person.

But, as David Brown points out:

> It is not the actual which the Christian values in another, but his potential, the fact that, as St Thomas put it, he is 'capable of eternal happiness'. That is why all human beings are of value irrespective of their actual conduct (e.g. Hitler) or their mental capacity (e.g. the mongoloid child).[3]

In other words, the human embryo is not a potential person, but a person with potential.

As far as the question of whether or not the embryo looks like a human person is concerned, David Brown rejects as 'nonsense' the notion that personhood should be identified with a particular physical structure.

> The Christian need only recall the persons of the Trinity, but even the non-Christian can be persuaded to adopt the same viewpoint. For he is constantly reminded by science fiction that personality need not depend on looking like a human being.[4]

The present writer believes that to exclude some human beings (in this case, embryos) from the moral status of personhood is to establish a grossly discriminatory attitude to certain people because it suits our interests. Christians have always believed in the sanctity of life. Whenever nations have varied from that principle they have embraced tyranny.

The alternative to accepting that personhood is an achievement is to accept that it is an endowment. We are valuable as human persons because we are human and not because we serve someone else's idea of functional usefulness. This, at least, ought to be clear to Christians, although it would appear that this is not always the case.

The Word of God took flesh of the Virgin Mary. That which was conceived in her 'is of the Holy Spirit'. When Mary visited Elizabeth, the child in Elizabeth's womb leapt for joy. From the moment of conception human life has been sanctified by God who created that life, and who has shared our human existence from the moment of conception.

This respect for the God-given nature of human life ought to be central to any Christian assessment of IVF. And if the human embryo has the moral status of any other human being, if it has a right to live as the most basic of all human rights, then the process of IVF cannot be accepted as ethically possible.

Particularly with the use of multiple embryos, the vast majority of human embryos are used and wasted in order to achieve a few pregnancies. The use of some persons for the benefit of others is an ethically wrong way to behave. We are not to use other people to suit our own interests or to safeguard our own personal happiness.

Even if only one embryo is made at a time and replaced in the uterus (the simple case) there is still only a 15 to 20 per cent chance of implantation. It is sometimes suggested that the simple case of one embryo is justified because there is a natural wastage of many embryos, as high as 50 to 75 per cent. The facts are that we do not really know what the natural wastage might be. And in any case it is irrelevant.

When human beings die naturally we do not imagine that we are responsible for their deaths. It is only when we kill, or behave so recklessly that we cause death, that we can speak of morally wrong actions and guilt for those actions. In the case of IVF we proceed, even to the simple case (which in practice is rarely if ever done), knowing that the procedure itself will occasion the deaths of 80 to 85 per cent of the selected embryos. This is to behave with a reckless indifference to the fate of those embryos in order to achieve a result that will be satisfactory to the interested parties. In addition there are the embryos which die, are washed down the sink, or are experimented on. There is, ethically speaking, a great difference between death by natural causes and death caused by human intervention.

Separation of conception from the marital act

The second main objection to IVF concerns the separation of pro-creation from sexual intercourse. This objection deals with the supplanting of sexual intercourse by laboratory fertilisation.

It should be said straight away that this objection is not born out of a distrust of any sort of scientific interference in our lives. It is not a question of IVF being unnatural. After all most medical procedures and treatments are, in that sense, non-natural.

Medical technology has a very important part to play in human affairs and therefore in overcoming infertility. However, this does not mean that every procedure is morally good or neutral. Nor does it follow that we should do something simply because we can do it.

However, IVF, as presently practised, is an exercise in the skilful production of people. It is not an expressive act of love. It is at once recognised that not all acts of natural conception come from acts of intercourse which are loving. Children can be born of sexual infidelity, lust or other forms of dehumanising behaviour between people.

However, IVF does not merely complete an act of intercourse by transferring semen, after intercourse, to the uterus. It takes the place of intercourse and is necessarily associated with the intervention of other people (scientists) in the conception of a child. In this sense the child comes into being as the end product of a process managed by people other than the parents, rather than as the result of sexual intercourse between husband and wife.

For some writers, such as Joseph Fletcher, laboratory fertilisation is to be preferred.

> A 'test tube baby', although conceived and gestated *ex corpo,* would nonetheless be humanly reproduced and of human value. A baby made artificially, by deliberate and careful contrivance, would be more human than one resulting from sexual roulette—the reproductive mode of the subhuman species.[5]

Conclusions

None of the above arguments should be taken to mean that the writer has no compassion for infertile couples. On the contrary, one sees it as a matter of great trauma for those involved. However, we must be careful not to see the solving of infertility (a test tube baby) as the only issue. The means by which infertility is overcome is also relevant. And the ends are not sufficient to justify the means.

IVF involves a radical disregard for human embryonic life, the implications of which ought not to be lost on the churches or on society at large. If the embryo has no moral status then we must accept the experimentation on embryos, including freezing, which may cause abnormalities, and the abortion of children of the IVF program diagnosed as abnormal. We will probably also accept abortion on request and possibly infanticide and euthanasia.

Already embryos are being made solely for the purposes of experimentation and with no intention to implant them in a woman.[6] If procreation is divorced from sexual intercourse what final argument can be brought against surrogate motherhood, wombs for rent, and the like?

Just as artificial insemination was developed for married couples but now involves exclusively the use of donor sperm, so now the move is towards IVF using eggs and sperm donated by strangers. If there is an accepted separation of procreation from intercourse how can we object to the use of donor gametes?

The right to a child is not an absolute right, and in any case ought not to be seen as higher than the right of the embryo to live and the need to safeguard the integrity and wholeness of marital sexual love.

There are alternatives to IVF. Firstly, prevention is better than cure. Damaged Fallopian tubes may be caused by a number of factors. High on the list of such causes are venereal diseases, sterilisation and abortion. We need to invest more time and effort into informing the community of the long-term consequence of sexual promiscuity and early sterilisation. Further, the possibility of mending damaged Fallopian tubes could be more fully explored and funded. Such procedures are not morally doubtful.

Above all there is a need for greater clarity on bioethical issues before the community is steamrollered into accepting IVF as a morally legitimate means for solving the infertility of women with damaged Fallopian tubes.

1   Dr J. N. Santamaria, 'The ethics and implications of in vitro fertilisation', August 1982.
2   'Indications of humanhood: a tentative profile of man', *The Hastings Center Report,* vol. 2, no. 5, November 1972.
3   *Choices: ethics and the Christian,* Blackwell, Oxford, 1983, p. 119.
4   ibid.
5   See note 2.
6   *Nature,* vol. 303, 25 May 1983.

7

Legal implications of the new reproductive technology

F. J. Brown

The Federal Attorney-General said recently that the Hawke Government 'recognised the dual role of law in simultaneously reflecting and moulding the social conscience of the community'.[1]

In discussing IVF and related matters, the Attorney's statement is a reminder of the number of perspectives from which the legal implications of developments in this area can be approached. It raises the Hart–Devline type debate on the relationship between morality and the law. One is also confronted with the question of the extent to which in a diverse society the law is a great educative force because it constitutes the only recognisable moral code. However, this contribution does not purport to deal with either of these substantial matters; rather its objective is far more mundane—to draw attention to some of the legal issues which IVF and associated developments raise.

The Attorney's statement is valuable because it makes us conscious of the fact that it is not possible to be objective in dealing with these sorts of issues. It is inevitable that one's values will permeate opinions offered and judgments made. Consequently, it is necessary at the outset that the writer declares his position.

This writer holds the view that personhood begins at conception. At conception embryos are complete. They require only food, warmth and shelter to reach their full potential. It is posited that to confer personhood at any other point in time is arbitrary. Attached to personhood is a variety of rights, the extent of which may be contested but which, it is submitted, must include the rights to live and not be experimented upon without a person's consent.

The word 'right' raises another perspective from which this subject might be approached—the relationship between legal rights, moral rights and natural rights. It is not the purpose of this chapter to consider that question. The writer recognises that the word 'right' raises important ethical and theological issues concerning whether matters of this sort ought to be considered from a basis of rights or obligations. The use of the word 'rights' in this limited contribution is for simplicity and does not necessarily reflect the writer's views on this question.

One of the procedures associated with IVF is AID, which has been with us for some time. As a result much attention has been given to certain legal problems (for example, inheritance) involving children one of whose parents is not the biological father. Much has been written on this subject and a recent meeting of Attorneys-General has acknowledged the need to legislate to deal with these matters. Consequently, this aspect of the implications of AID is not dealt with in this chapter.

This chapter is written at the time the Victorian Government has announced its intention to allow the IVF program to proceed. It proposes to enact legislation in 1984. Since details of the legislation are not available, it is not possible to take the Victorian Government's decision into account at this juncture.

By way of preliminaries, it is worth recalling the position of the law with respect to life before birth from an historical point of view. In the seventeenth century Sir Edward Coke, reflecting the then current position, said that the law did not recognise life prior to birth. While some may argue that is still the position at common law, it is submitted that such a statement would be inaccurate today. The historic plea of *en ventre sa mère* constituted an action whereby the courts treated the unborn child as though it were born. This principle was enacted in the United Kingdom in 1931 with the passing of the Sentence of Death (Expectant Mothers) Act, which provided for the commutation of a sentence of death on an expectant mother.

In recent years, we have seen a number of decisions resulting from abortion cases. Among the better known is the United States Supreme Court decision in *Roe* v. *Wade* (410 US 113 (1973)), in which the court held the state's interest in protecting life becomes compelling when a foetus reaches 'the interim point at which (it is) . . . potentially able to live outside the mother's womb albeit with artificial aid'. (However, a recent decision indicates that this decision is not the court's final say on the issue.)[2]

Further developments have occurred with respect to injury cases. The law has gone from the position outlined by Coke to the decision of the Victorian Supreme Court in *Watt* v. *Rama* ([1972] VR 353), where a child recovered damages resulting from an accident when the child was a foetus not more than 4 weeks old.

The *Roe* v. *Wade* viability test is worth considering in the light of the current rapid developments. Early in 1982 most people interested in the IVF program would have said that this decision could not be used to protect the blastocyst. Yet by the end of the year Dr Edwards of Edwards and Steptoe fame had admitted he had been able to keep a blastocyst alive for 4 days. At this stage, most would still say the *Roe* v. *Wade* test is still irrelevant, but what does the future hold in store?

An early issue raised by IVF is the status of the surplus embryo. Professor Singer offered this opinion:

> If you're asking a legal question, I'm not sure that anybody knows because the law hasn't dealt with this sort of case before. If you're asking an ethical question, I think it is really up to the hospital ethics committee what is going to happen to them.[3]

The position of those who argue that rights begin at conception is simple—don't have surplus embryos. Their problem is a practical one—enforcement. For those of a different view, the question is far from academic where freezing occurs. A substantial number of marriages finish in the divorce court. In those cases what happens to surplus embryos? Should all embryos automatically be destroyed regardless of the wishes of the parties? Alternatively, should the decision rest with hospital ethics committees as suggested by Professor Singer? Should it be left to the courts? Maybe the criterion should be consent. If the prospective parents can agree on the embryo's future (that is, destruction or ownership passes to either party or to a third party or institution), then their decision prevails. On the other hand if they cannot agree then the fate of the embryo might rest with the divorce courts in exactly the same way that all other forms of property are dealt with by the courts. However, we could respond to Professor Singer's suggestion or maybe even leave it to the doctors and technicians.

Associated with the question of divorce is the question of separation. Some would say that in this case decisions are even more difficult. The issues are those that have been outlined above. However, there is an added factor. Should the separation be considered permanent? Should criteria be developed so that permanence can be determined? Should the question of permanence even be considered?

A canvassing of various scenarios must include the implications of death. Does the embryo become the property of the survivor to dispose of as he or she wishes? If the wife is the survivor may she, subsequent to the death of her husband, have the embryo implanted? Should there be provision for pre-signed statements indicating the wishes of spouses in these circumstances? Again one asks whether there should be mandatory destruction, whether ownership should pass to a hospital in these circumstances or whether ethics committees ought to make the appropriate decisions.

Of course these questions make certain assumptions, especially that any laws, rules, regulations or guidelines are enforceable. Such an assumption cannot be made. These questions are pointless unless there is a comprehensive and mandatory recording of details of all surplus embryos. Whether such a recording can be made without a central embryo bank is worth pondering. Whether one could verify the implementation of any decisions (for example, destruction or embryo transfer) without a central bank is questionable. Whether the relevant authority could rely upon people to inform it of those circumstances about which it would need to know is problematical.

If it is thought that these situations notwithstanding their numbers still represent the exception, one can turn to 'normal' scenarios. Could surplus embryos be sold? If so, should the purposes for which the embryos are used be restricted? For example, should there be a prohibition on sales for the purpose of experimentation? If there are to be any prohibitions, how does one rationalise such a prohibition with the idea of 'wastage'? After all if it is possible to destroy an embryo, why is it not possible to sell it?

Of course all of these matters raise the most fundamental issue—ownership. Again, for those who say that rights are enjoyed from conception, there is a clear answer. Ownership of one person by another went out with the slave trade. The answer is equally as clear for those who argue that persons do not have any absolute rights. However, their difficulty is the legal position. In Victoria, where common law prevails, not only absolute rights are recognised, but rights are accorded to the foetus by restricting the legality of abortions to those situations where it is: (a) necessary to preserve the woman from serious danger to her life or her physical or mental health (not being merely the normal dangers of pregnancy and childbirth) which the continuance of the pregnancy would entail; and

(b) in the circumstances not out of proportion to the danger to be averted (*R.* v. *Davidson* [1969] VR 667). Although this decision is not directly related to the embryo before implantation it does carry overtones of rights from conception.

The real problem exists for those who contend that rights begin at a point subsequent to conception. It is posited that with recent developments in IVF and related fields it is no longer feasible to argue that the accrual of rights by embryos and foetuses is an evolving period without specifying at which point in time which rights accrue. Once these matters have been determined, the next question is what is the status of the embryo or foetus before that point in time. If the embryo is not a person then the answer is simple, although the logic of saying one day that a foetus is not a person, and the next day he or she is, is rather mystifying. The embryo is a chattel and like any chattel can be disposed of as the owners see fit, subject to any legal restrictions which may be imposed. It merely remains to determine whether ownership vests in the couple, the hospital, the medical team or some central bank. However, if the embryo prior to this point is considered to be a person without any rights, serious issues are raised. Does that mean that we are philosophically speaking returning to the pre-Wilberforce days? Alternatively, does it suggest that the right not to be owned by another person is a right which is not intrinsic, but rather which is acquired? If so, does such a position have implications for any other categories of person within society?

Problems would emerge if an administrative error is made. For example, it might be that the wrong embryo is destroyed. Hospital authorities in Australia will be hoping that events in the United States are not a sign of things to come. In *Del Zio* v. *Presbyterian Hospital* an action for damages for pain and suffering suffered as the result of the deliberate destruction of a blastocyst was successful.

Equally as difficult is the situation where an administrative bungle occurs and a wrong embryo is implanted. Should an action lie if the operation is not successful on the basis that it may have been successful if the right embryo had been implanted? In the event that the child resulting from the implanting of the wrong embryo has a defect or handicap should an action lie? At the other end, should the parents of an embryo which is wrongly implanted be able to maintain an action?

The suggestion of legal actions in these situations raises the question of the grounds on which an action might be instituted. The same issue must be confronted when asking whether an action would lie in the event that an IVF or AID child is born with a defect, impediment or handicap. Presumably, there would be an obligation on those involved (that is, doctors, hospitals and clinics and staff) to use the reasonable care and skill of professionals exercising their particular expertise. However, the onus of proof that a sufficient degree of skill and care was not used would rest with the parents or child as the case may be.

In the case of an AID child there is the further question of whether an action lies and against whom in the event of genetic defect. By virtue of the duty to take reasonable care the donor presumably is required to disclose details of diseases from which he suffers and of which he is aware. However, to what extent should doctors etc. make inquiries in order to discharge their duty to take care? Of course this discussion assumes that records of donors are available—an invalid assumption at the moment. If records are not available should the hospital, clinic or doctor be automatically liable for any genetic defect?

It would seem that the destruction of embryos before implantation is not an offence. Section 65 of the Victorian *Crimes Act* 1958 deals with unlawful miscarriages.[4] Until implantation occurs, a miscarriage cannot be procured. The position is anomalous.

The possibility of surrogate motherhood raises a range of complex issues. First, there is the case where a woman agrees to carry and give birth to an embryo fertilised by a couple for a fee. If the contract provides for the woman to subject herself to foetal monitoring for the purpose of causing an abortion if abnormalities appear, and she refuses, what happens? Alternatively, if she subjects herself to the monitoring but refuses to have an abortion, should this breach of contract require a mandatory abortion, payment of damages or merely that the woman be required to keep the child without support from the couple?

The other side of the coin is that the woman decides to have an abortion because of foetal abnormality. What action is available to the couple? What remedy should be available? If the monitoring reveals abnormality who determines whether there should be an abortion—the woman or the couple?

Assuming the child survives until birth, the problems do not cease. The woman may refuse to hand the child back to the couple. The couple may refuse to take custody of the child. Custody of children has been based on what is considered to be the best interests of the child. However, how would the principle be applied, especially if nobody wanted the child?

The other, and presently more common, surrogate motherhood situation is where the wife is infertile and the husband contributes semen for an AID child from another woman. One can pose the same questions but the fact that the woman is the biological mother may lead to different answers.

In considering the implications of surrogate motherhood, the British decision, *Paton* v. *Trustees of BPAS* ([1978] 2 All ER 987), where it was held that a man could not prevent his wife from having an abortion, is interesting. It has been suggested that on the basis of that decision the biological mother has as much standing vis-à-vis the surrogate mother as the father vis-à-vis the mother when considering having an abortion. However, the British Abortion Act 1967 does refer to 'the pregnant woman'. Whether that sufficiently distinguishes legislation such as the Victorian Crimes Act which refers to 'any woman' would need to be considered.

Finally, we turn to the question of experimentation on embryos. Today there appears to be a legal vacuum which could allow open slather. In various states of the United States there are laws which specifically deal with prohibitions on experimentation. However, the position in Australia is different. The recent admissions of freezing embryos are an example. While many are eulogising the benefits of modern science, clearly scientists experimented with freezing embryos until they developed the 'right technique'.

Recently in the *Attorney-General for the State of Queensland on the relation of David Lindsay Kerr* v. *Miss T,* the Chief Justice of the High Court 'agree[d] with the judgment of Sir George Baker in *Paton* v. *Trustees of BPAS* that a foetus has no right of its own until it is born and has a separate existence from its mother'. As already noted above, Dr Edwards has admitted to keeping a blastocyst alive for 4 days. Experimentation by freezing has been conducted in Victoria. There would not appear to be any law against the destruction of embryos. The question is: why in these circumstances should one not allow and what is there to prevent cloning?

This chapter is not exhaustive. It does not purport to provide answers. At the very least is has attempted to highlight Mr Justice Kirby's statement:

> The one thing that is plain is that the law on this topic is not a matter to be drafted behind closed doors by committees, however expert and sincere. It is certainly not a matter for doctors and scientists only or lawyers alone. It is not a matter for university scholars working in their offices or individual researchers. It is not a matter for hospital ethics committees. If there is a need for profound and thoughtful community debate on an issue, this is it.[5]

1   Address to the Second National Environmental Law Symposium held in Melbourne on 21 October 1983.

2   In the *City of Akron* v. *Akron Centre for Reproductive Health,* the
United States Supreme Court held certain provisions concerning access
to and the performing of abortions unconstitutional, but Justices White,
Rehnquist and O'Connor attacked trimester analysis, which underpins
the *Roe* v. *Wade* decision. In *Planned Parenthood Association of Kan-
sas City, Missouri* v. *Ashcroft,* which also concerns matters pertaining to
abortion, a majority of the Supreme Court held certain provisions constitutional while a minority, Justices O'Connor, White and Rehnquist,
considered all provisions constitutional and Justice Blackman, the authority of the *Roe* v. *Wade* decision, considered all provisions unconstitutional.

3   TV interview by Terry Lane, 'Pippin—a very special child', April 1982.

4   The law with respect to abortion is not uniform throughout Australia.
The position in Victoria and New South Wales is determined by common law and is similar. However, in South Australia, for example, the
law is governed by statute and in Queensland, while common law prevails, there is not an equivalent of the Menhennit or Levine rulings.

5   *Medical Journal of Australia,* 11 July 1981.

8

Issues for the family

Alan Nichols

Everyone grew up in a family of some kind, and feels familiar with the security, protection and sense of belonging that goes with it. At the same time, we are constantly told that the family shape is changing, and that perhaps the concept of the family is dissolving into something entirely different.

The fact is that the family is here to stay, despite pressures from within and without. The 1981 census showed that 85 per cent of Australians were living in families. The remainder were living alone (5.8 per cent), living with other non-related persons (5.1 per cent) or not living in a private dwelling (4.5 per cent).

What is more, despite the variety of family forms these days, 60 per cent of the Australian population do in fact live in conventional, two-parent nuclear families.[1] As well, there are many families of couples without children who are transitional versions of the traditional nuclear family; that is, they are couples who will have children in the future, or whose children have left home.

The reason why the family survives so well is that it is the natural set of relationships within which children grow to maturity and adults find security and personal development. This could be put in terms of theology, but social research and even government inquiries bear it out. The Victorian Government's Child Welfare Practice and Legislation Review Committee recently came to this conclusion[2], echoing the finding of the Commonwealth Government's Royal Commission on Human Relationships a few years back.[3]

It is the nurturing, protecting and identity roles of the family which become important in the bioethical debates. For both artificial insemination and in vitro fertilisation create 'artificial families'. What happens within those families and how they relate to the Australian social fabric of family life become very important questions which may dictate whether whole biomedical programs, or some parts of them, should continue at all. They are not just private questions affecting only the infertile couples involved, together with their medical advisers or genetic counsellors. The whole Australian community has an interest.

The marriage relationship

Since the family fractures when the marriage breaks down, let us look first at the pressures brought on the infertile marriage by the introduction of third or fourth parties by AID or IVF by donor.

As Gareth Jones has pointed out:

> AID introduces into the family unit only half an outsider, namely a child carrying the wife's genes but not the husband's. In this regard the child is more part of the family than an adopted child. However, in order to accomplish this, a biological bond between the husband and wife has been severed. AID involves the radical separation of marriage and parenthood.[4]

Once procreation has been subdivided in such a way that part of it can be technologically reproduced in a laboratory, and a third party introduced, it can be argued that the integrity of human parenthood is lost. It becomes a question of weighing the desirability of having a biological child to nurture against the undesirability of a third party's intervention. It needs to be a strong marriage, not only in the mutual relationship, but also in the capacity to handle the husband's continuing infertility while raising the child of another as his own.

The problem is greatly exacerbated when a fourth party is introduced into this biological–technological process, as in the case of donor sperm and donor ova. The child so produced is not the biological child of either parent, at the point of procreation, but it is of course nurtured in the womb. If surrogate motherhood becomes a possibility, then you can have a fifth party involved, if both sperm and ova are donated.

In all these circumstances, assuming that all these procedures become approved and go ahead (a matter still under investigation by State government committees in New South Wales, Queensland and Victoria), counselling becomes an absolute esssential. This counselling must be not only about the genetic and medical questions, but also about the strength of the marriage relationship, the identity of the child, and the sense of belonging together of the future family unit.

The recommendations therefore of the Victorian government committee on counselling must be strongly supported. These are that 'comprehensive information, including ethical, social, psychological and legal matters bearing on all aspects of the treatment of infertility, should be available to all infertile couples'.[5]

The strains that infertility causes in marriages should not be under-estimated. For example, it has been estimated in England that the process of screening AID applicants has resulted in a lower divorce rate among them than in the population as a whole.[6] But AID and IVF have the potential to increase stress within the relationship. One reason is the inequality of relationship between child and parents, where the husband is not physically responsible for conception in the same way as the wife. The Feversham Report in the U.K.[7] thought that the child might be a continual reminder to the husband of his 'inadequacy'. Not much research has been done on AID families, but Snowden and Mitchell did find resentment in some marriages, with strains on the relationship.[8] A couple wanting donor AID or IVF must be very sure that a lack of paternity will not be used at a later stage by either partner to undermine relationships within the family.

For this reason, counselling should be not only before the medical process, but afterwards, as is the usual practice in Victorian adoption agencies. Because legalisation of an adoption occurs about twelve months after the child is placed, there is a built-in reason for calling on, encouragement and counselling of the new family unit while it undergoes the early strains of adjustment.

Such follow-up and pastoral care should not be left to professionals. For one thing, that keeps it in the realm of the medical. For another, the best kind of care is 'amateur', neighbourhood and family support occurring naturally in most Australian suburbs and country towns. Infant welfare sisters, local churches, community groups and schools could be more alert to the opportunity of supporting the 'artificial families' created by AID and IVF. The publicity, novelty and biological differences may be adding strains which other people could alleviate.

Openness in the family

An essential ingredient in any family which is going to survive under all the contemporary pressures is openness and frankness. Any secrecy about a child's procreation or biological origin produces stress not only in the early years, but on a continuing basis if the secret is going to be kept. This stress is worse if adults in the family circle know the secret, but the child does not. This is documented in U.K. studies[9] and in Australian adoption practice.[10]

Snowden and Mitchell found quite conclusively about AID children:

> We have found it necessary to indicate that in so far as AID may be a threat to normal families and may arouse uncertainty in children's minds about their origins, and most particularly in so far as it usually does entail secrecy, it is undermining the social values of openness, honesty and truthfulness on which social institutions and the institutional behaviour we know as family life rests.[11]

It would seem logical that they would also come to the same conclusions about children born by IVF using donor gametes.

The secrecy is in two areas: whether the child knows its biological origins and the technological process; and whether there is access to information about the donor(s). 'Who were my father *and* my mother?' would be the question when both donor sperm and ova are used. Hence, the Victorian government committee has recommended very specifically not only that donors' records be kept in a central registry, but that information on request should be supplied in a way which does not cause any confusion about identity.[12] This information however would not include the actual name and address of the donor, but only such medical and other information as would be useful. It is quite different from the proposals under consideration by the same State Government about access to name and address of relinquishing mothers and putative fathers on the request of adoptees, if all the parties agree.[13] If adoptees have rights to their origins (all parties agreeing), why not AID and IVF children? The issues are the same. The reason for caution is of course to protect adults who may not wish to be contacted years later and faced with a child which has been forgotten or even never met. But the reason for the search is obvious: children, especially from puberty and into adulthood, want to know where they came from.

It is clearly critical for openness within the family that children are told, at an appropriate age, that they are AID or IVF children. This has been a requirement by adoption agencies of applicants for adoption for many years. It should be an automatic part of the AID and IVF procedures also.

Identity of the child

It is impossible to separate the openness question from the identity question. Although U.K. adoption research has shown that only about 1 per cent of adult adoptees search actively for their origins, it is very important for that 1 per cent to have legal rights in that search. This is to be recognised in Victorian adoption legislation for adoptees 18 years of age and over. It should be recognised in any AID and IVF legislation.

This parallel between IVF and adoption practice was recognised by the Victorian government committee:

> There is, in the committee's opinion, a substantial and growing view that the values of honesty and integrity are crucial to the creation of a happy family. In adoption practice it is now almost universal for the adopting parents to be counselled that they should tell the adopted child of its background. Great care has been given to the development of sensitive approaches which parents may use for this purpose. There is a similar development in some counselling which is provided for participants in AID programs, although it is recognised that the considerations are not exactly the same as in adoption.[14]

That committee recommended that a central registry should be established and controlled by the Health Commission to retain comprehensive information about donors whose gametes have been successfully used in an IVF program. This registry should also contain details of successful pregnancies and of any abnormalities found in a child born through the donor program.

The availability of non-identifying genetic information in this way will go a long way towards assisting the search for identity of any IVF child, and therefore should assist the whole family in coping with the identity crisis a child may go through at the point of discovery. This moment of discovery can be harrowing for the child[15], but maintaining secrecy can be worse.

A further complication in the identity of an IVF child would be if he/she is born into a single parent household or into a lesbian relationship. The Victorian government inquiry looked briefly at the possibility of de facto relationships but felt that it should limit itself to married couples. It did not consider IVF for lesbians or single women.

However, it is known that single women and lesbian couples have had children through AID. As Snowden and Mitchell have pointed out[17], 'some practitioners are willing to provide AID for single women whilst others abhor the idea'. On the basic principle that AID and IVF have justification only when they are technological means of overcoming infertility, there seems to be no justification for providing the service for single women or lesbians. The whole experience of family welfare also supports the view that children deserve to have as nurturers two parents, one of each sex, if at all possible.[18]

Surrogate mothers

At least in both AID and IVF the child is actually nurtured in the womb until born. There develops in that period a sense of belonging, of care and nurture. This pre-birth experience is supported by the early nurture after birth which provides essential mother–child bonding without which a child is deprived sometimes seriously disadvantaged.

It is for this reason—quite apart from any absolute moral standpoint—that surrogate motherhood must be opposed. For another woman to bear the child, which is after birth 'adopted' by the parents who may have provided either sperm or ova, runs counter to all the present knowledge on bonding and nurture.

Surrogate motherhood would also greatly complicate the sense of personal identity in the child. 'Who indeed is my mother?' These concerns would surely overwhelm the medical reasons advanced by Professor Carl Wood[19] for considering use of a surrogate. He acknowledges difficulties around use of surrogates, but looks forward to the community gradually coming around to approving of the idea, if the lawyers can find solutions to the obvious legal problems of ownership. The essence of the problem is not, in my opinion, legal, but ethical.

Questions

In my view the following questions need to be explored and satisfactorily answered before the use of donors in AID or IVF should be sanctioned:

Does secrecy have harmful effects within the extended family of those involved?

Should relationships within the wider AID or IVF family be the subject of follow-up pastoral care and of long-term research?

Do relatives of the IVF child and couple have a right to knowledge about the child's origin?

How far is adoption a model for AID and IVF practice?

What is the likely effect of increasing use of IVF on the children of other families?

Does the use of donors in AID and IVF constitute a danger to the institutions of marriage and family?

What are the likely effects of IVF being available to single women or lesbian couples?

1   Peter McDonald, Institute of Family Studies, article in *Australian Society,* December 1983.

2   Interim Report of the Child Welfare Practice and Legislation Review Committee, November 1983, p. 5.

3   *Royal Commission on Human Relationships Final Report,* AGPS, Canberra, 1976, vol. 1, pp. 63, 110.

4   Gareth Jones, *Genetic engineering,* Grove Books, Bramcote, 1978, p. 18.

5   *Report on donor gametes in IVF* of Committee to Consider the Social, Ethical and Legal Issues arising from In Vitro Fertilisation, Victoria, August 1983, p. 42.

6   David Ison, *Artificial insemination by donor,* Grove Books, Bramcote, 1983, p. 9.

7   *Report of the Departmental Committee on Human Artificial Insemination* (Feversham Report), HMSO, London, 1960, p. 38.

8   R. Snowden & G. D. Mitchell, *The artificial family,* Allen & Unwin, London, 1981, p. 39.

9   Snowden & Mitchell, p. 121.

10   Submission of Adoption Section, Mission of St James and St John, August 1982, to Victorian government inquiry into IVF.

11   Snowden & Mitchell, p. 121.

12   *Report on donor gametes in IVF,* p. 46.

13   Victorian Government Adoption Legislation Review Committee Report, 1983.

14   *Report on donor gametes in IVF,* p. 26.

15   Snowden & Mitchell, p. 88.

16   *Report on donor gametes in IVF,* p. 35.

17   Snowden & Mitchell, p. 122.

18   Professor Urie Bronfenbrenner of Cornell University, U.S., at Macquarie University seminar 1982, 'Children and families: the silent revolution'.

19   Professor Carl Wood & Ann Westmore, *Test-tube conception,* Hill of Content, Melbourne, 1983, p. 113.

9

Pastoral care dimensions

Roy Bradley

For a useful beginning to our understanding of the nature of pastoral care we turn to the introduction to Ministration to the Sick in An Australian Prayer Book. There, we note, 'Pastoral care as a ministry of the Gospel occurs when the love of God sustains people experiencing specific needs and stresses. The relation between the pastor and the sick person is of the first importance in this ministry'. Let me expand this introduction, in which we learn that pastoral care is personal and relational. I will do this under three separate titles, viz. Being there, Being ourselves and Pastoral care as evangelism.

Being there

Much is said in training programs for professional health care workers about the necessity to avoid over-involvement with the client. The importance of maintaining appropriate distance so as to be as objective as possible is stressed over and over. It is a valid point and in pastoral care we would want to avoid the situation where the object of our concern is simply a vehicle for enhancing our own self-esteem, or working through our own problems. Nor do we wish to lose the capacity of discernment and the ability to set appropriate limits on the demands made on us. Yet if we are to remain true servants of Jesus Christ the call to reach out is ever present. Jesus makes it quite clear that he is to be identified as the servant whose work is so sublimely portrayed in Isaiah 61 (see also Luke 4:16−21).

From Isaiah we learn that the work of the servant includes establishing justice, making a special covenant with God's people, preaching good tidings, revealing God to the nations, healing the broken-hearted, releasing those who are in bondage, comforting those who mourn, and making it possible not only to be renewed here but to enjoy the hope of eternal life. It is a formidable task and its claim on us does not lessen in its intensity with the passing of the years, nor with changing circumstances.

Servanthood is not slavery. It is a willingness to commit oneself to a cause. In this context that cause is the frontier of existence where people are isolated and hurting as they face the ambiguities and hazards of life. I am certain it is that claim of others that has always drawn men and women out of the relative security of their own mode of living (see Isaiah 6:8). The pastor is the one man:

> . . . who cannot be permitted the luxury of a sheltered life. Nothing indicates more clearly the ministry's betrayal of its functions than the growth of the widespread notion that parsons are plants too sensitive to bear the rigours of life in the world as it is and have to be sheltered against its blasts.[1]

Henri Nouwen gives a clue as to the purpose of our involvement. He claims that:

> When one has the courage to enter where life is experienced as most unique and most private, one touches the soul of the community. The man who has spent many hours trying to understand, feel and clarify the alienation and confusion of one of his fellow men might well be the best equipped to speak to the needs of the many, for all men are one at the well-spring of pain and joy.

Implicit in this reaching out is a fundamental respect for the pre-eminence of persons. Respect in itself infers valuing or esteeming the intrinsic worth of a person. Another way of stating that is the unconditional acceptance of the other, for as Paul Tournier reminds us:

> Love and Christian charity do not lie in discussing and arguing with people to persuade them of something, but in loving them and accepting them.[3]

We will expand this thought later but right now a fundamental respect for others also means a fundamental respect of their need to keep secrets about themselves.

The inclusion of values takes us deeper into the web of pastoral relationships. All of our behaviour is influenced by values, attitudes and assumptions, and while these remain unexamined, conflicts and distortions in relationships will prevail. In my early days in hospital chaplaincy I remember once interceding for a 60-year-old widow who was admitted to hospital with a severe blood disorder six months after her husband had died. Convinced there was a strong link between her deteriorating health and an unresolved grief reaction, I sought an extension of her hospitalisation to counsel her. I was not prepared for the resident doctor's response, however. 'Why waste your time on someone who has, at the most, only ten more years to live?' he argued. In hindsight, of course, my indignation was unjustified. I could have arranged a series of out-patient appointments, referred her to her local minister or even called on her at home.

Honest, open and frank discussion is possible when there is an atmosphere of acceptance. And where health care teams meet regularly and the representatives from the various health professions are not caught up in the struggle for power, or hell-bent on ego trips, effective communication is possible. On reflection, considering our individual and varied backgrounds, even our peculiar family customs, and our training, the wonder is that we communicate at all, for communication by definition means sharing something in common. It has also been described as a 'meeting of meaning'.[4]

Honesty and openness are just two facilitators of communication. There is a third and it probably precedes the other two in importance. It is *listening*.[5] It is a given fact of life that when someone feels they have been truly listened to, they will also feel valued, and, as a result, affirmed. We should not dismiss too lightly the therapeutic, i.e. life-giving, quality of affirmation. There is another side to this coin. Some people do not want to be listened to for to be heard is to be known and that is too threatening for some. The basis of so much of the inhibition that interferes with the development of effective and meaningful pastoral relationships is to be found right here.

> I realise that when I do not love myself I may be rejecting the love of God, saying that I know better than the Divine Lover, that I am not lovable or capable of being loved.[6]

People generally want to tell the truth about themselves, though in order to do so they often resort to the use of what Elizabeth Kubler-Ross calls 'symbolic language'. Listening with the 'third ear' the sensitive pastor will be attuned to the inner meaning that lies behind the outward verbal expression.

So then, for the pastor, involvement in the form of reaching out to men and women who are isolated from significantly meaningful relationships comes to be seen to include a sense of commitment to the acceptance of the other, with keen respect for the other's privacy, and the willingness to take time and expend energy to listen to the other. When those elements are present it can be said that the relationship takes on the form of a covenant.[7] We saw earlier that it was the task of the servant to establish a covenant between God and his people ('They will be my people and I will be their God', Ezekiel 11:20, Zechariah 8:8). It is this element of faithfulness that distinguishes the covenant relationship from the contractual one.

> In the covenant there is no condition put on faithfulness. It is the unconditional commitment to be of service.[8]

Being ourselves

It is clear from our comments about involvement that persons who are the objects of our pastoral care are not thereby objects to be manipulated at will. Nor are they objects in the sense that they are our possession. They are not 'my' patients, for example. Nor indeed are they objects in the sense that they can be labelled, least of all stereotyped. No other attitude does more harm to the development of a genuine encounter with the other than does stereotyping. 'He's an alcoholic, and you know you can't do much for alcoholics' is but one example. Lastly, the pastor is not called to make decisions for others, nor to shield them from the responsibilities which are theirs. In other words, pastoral care is a person-centred ministry not a problem-solving one.

Yet it can never be as clear cut as that. Once again it is Jesus who restores the balance: 'Would any of you who are fathers give your son a stone when he asks for bread?' (Matthew 7:9). Nothing could be more simple than that. When men are hungry we feed them. When men are victims of an oppressive economic system that robs them of employment we support them, and their right to be gainfully employed. And when men are hungering after righteousness, we offer them 'the way' insofar and inasmuch as we have discovered it to be so for ourselves (see below).

Pastoral care is not a matter of specific acts that one does for another person. or a set of basic principles which are applied in a number of different circumstances. This does not negate the need for training, for learning certain basic skills, especially if a pastor would also want to engage in formal counselling. Even so, training without the three essential ingredients of accurate empathy, non-possessive warmth and genuineness does little to enhance the character of the pastor's own human presence. The value of our care lies not so much in what we say, nor in what we do, but rather in who we are.[9]

Thus, the person of the pastor is a significant factor in pastoral care. How can he best make use of his person in the service of another? Sidney Jourard declares that effective therapists seem to follow this implicit hypothesis:

> If they are themselves in the presence of the patient, if they let the patient
> and themselves be, avoiding compulsions to silence, to reflection, to in-
> terpretation . . . but instead striving to know their patient, involving them-
> selves in his situation and then responding to his utterances with their
> spontaneous selves, this fosters growth.[10]

Being ourselves does not mean saying or doing what we feel like
in the act of caring. Freedom is not licence. Being ourselves means
that we are functioning as free, genuine and responsible persons.
Being ourselves means that we take seriously the necessity to keep
our own house in order and be open to change. Finally, being ourselves means that we are sufficiently in touch with our strengths, skills
and resources that we know when and how to use them, without
contrivance, in the service of the other.

In practical terms this attitude will be reflected in a number of ways
in the actual encounter with the other, as follows:

(1) The pastor has no false picture about his own finiteness, and
   will not hesitate to admit when he is wrong.

(2) The pastor is well aware that he cannot offer an environment of
   nurturing care if he has not already experienced loving acceptance himself.

(3) The pastor will not be afraid to share his own experience of life.

He knows that his own personality and frame of reference, influenced as it is by his own value system and understanding of the
person of man, will act as a signpost to others. To pretend otherwise
is to fly in the face of a vast storehouse of experience in one-to-one
therapeutic relationships. Carl Rogers says:

> What is most personal and unique in each one of us is probably the very
> element which would, if it were shared or expressed, speak most deeply to
> others.[11]

There is always an element of risk in any relationship. Hopefully in
the pastoral context what may start out as a duel will eventually end
up as a duet! Let Bonhoeffer have the last word: 'He who gives care
also receives it'.

Pastoral care as evangelism

If it is true that all therapeutic agents aspire to help persons change
the course of their lives, then I cannot see why there is so much
resistance to equating pastoral care with evangelism. Obviously, the
well-versed practitioner of pastoral care is not going to violate his
relationship with another by proselytising, i.e. setting out with the deliberate intention of making a convert of the other. Evangelism, for

my purposes here, has more to do with proclamation, but not in the sense of preaching. There is no place in a pastoral encounter for sermonising. But if we have agreed it is appropriate to share our life experience then the Christian pastor quite naturally and without deviousness will want to share those parts of that experience which have helped him make sense out of nonsense of the world. If this is accepted then the pastor is at liberty to confront the inconsistencies of rationalised behaviour, 'expose the hidden purposes of people's minds'[12], and to encourage the development of that attitude which is prepared to take seriously the symbolic and mystical occurrences that are part of our life experience, but that require a particular sensitivity to appreciate. Furthermore, he will encourage the acceptance of the truth that there are some things in this life we cannot change, our mortality being the most obvious. Finally, if there is one believable fragment of the creation myth it surely is the question God puts to Adam, viz. 'Where are you?' (Genesis 3:8–10). Ultimately, the question requires an answer from us all. Where are we in relation to God, in relation to ourselves, in relation to others and in relation to his creation? When we take those questions seriously we may find ourselves a fraction more meditative about some of the decisions we have to make.

Pastoral counselling

While I believe the insights and practical wisdom outlined above are the foundation stones of all pastoral care, I do not imagine they are all in evidence in every act of pastoral caring. Some situations or circumstances of life which are temporarily immobilising do not require anything more than simple common sense. Others, however, demand a competence which comes only from extensive training and experience. Furthermore, counselling does not necessarily require long-term care for it to be effective. The successful outcome is dependent rather on the resources and motivation of the person to be counselled and the ability of the counsellor to facilitate their mobilisation.

It is necessary now I believe to be reminded of an important truth posited by Don S. Browning. He claims:

> Care goes on in a cultural context of some kind. When a practitioner is oblivious to this fact there is likely to be an exaggeration of the technical and scientific aspects of care and a blindness to the cultural assumptions, symbols and goals that define the actual horizons of care.[13]

Is this an accurate description of the IVF and ET scene in Melbourne today? William Walters and Peter Singer appear to have no doubts about the answer to that question.[14] But is an ethics committee close enough to the clinical base to safeguard against the kind of bias indicated by Browning? Judging by the content of recent media releases it would certainly not seem to be so.

Is there an alternative? I believe the inclusion of an experienced and clinically trained chaplain in the health care team attached to the clinic would be a first step. Browning maintains the church, after all, is the historic bearer of an 'ethical sensibility that permeates the larger society'.[15] To overlook that heritage is to call into disrepute the church's highly significant impact on the cultural norms of our society. Hence Browning argues:

> How to enter into sensitive moral inquiry with troubled and confused individuals without becoming moralistic is, I contend, the major technical and methodological task for training in pastoral care in the future.[16]

Before that state of affairs is possible, however, it is necessary to reiterate that where IVF and ET procedures are in vogue, a health care team which is truly representative of all the caring professions should be an absolute priority. Such a group has a capacity to convict each participant of powerlessness which the one-to-one relationship commonly hides from them. It also has the potential for mutual support, for breaking down prejudices, for shared responsibility and shared accountability; in brief, for setting limits on extravagances and abuses of power. I wish to make it quite clear that I am in no way critical of the medical practitioner's judgment in this highly specialised field. Nor would I imagine that the element of 'sour grapes' is anything but a rare phenomenon. As has been intimated, a clinically trained chaplain would not feel intimidated by the aura surrounding his professional counterpart. Who knows, that same medical practitioner may be waiting to hear the chaplain express opinions to which he is entitled by virtue of his own training, experience and position on the team. Finally, the team that functions authentically is the one that also considers the tougher decisions. These may include, for example, fostering the adaptability of the couple to contend with their infertility. While it is the proper function of the medical practitioner to diagnose infertility, it is questionable whether his training would equip him to help couples consider alternatives to intervention. It will always make a profound difference if our various starting points are not the subject of corporate scrutiny. That, as I have said, must be the first item on the agenda of the health care team.

While the chaplain is quite familiar with the range of emotions experienced in relation to a crisis, no matter what its origin, e.g. shock, denial, isolation, anger, guilt, depression, grief and acceptance[17], he may not be as familiar with the complexities of an infertility clinic. To have a working knowledge of the techniques used, likely outcomes including possible side effects of treatment, as well as the implications of decisions made, let alone mastering the jargon, will take months of patient learning. Yet it must be done; for unless the church is directly involved through her representative at the clinical level where medicine is engaged in such radically innovative techniques, she will continue to experience resistance, even resentment and hostility, to her viewpoint.

1   Frank Lake, *Clinical theology,* Darton Longman & Todd, 1966.

2   Henri J. M. Nouwen, *The wounded healer,* Doublebay & Co.

3   From the transcript of an address given in Chicago, U.S.A., 30 March 1965.

4   Reuel Howe, *The miracle of dialogue* (publisher unknown).

5   Morton T. Kelsey, *Caring,* Paulist Press, 1981.

6   ibid., p. 53.

7   Henri J. M. Nouwen, *Creative ministry,* Doublebay & Co., 1978.

8   ibid.

9   For opportunities in clinical pastoral education address all inquiries to the Secretary, Association for Supervised Pastoral Education in Australia, Austin Hospital, Heidelberg, Vic. 3084.

10 Sidney M. Jourard, *The transparent self,* D. Van Nostrand Co., 1971.

11 Quoted by Henri J. M. Nouwen in *The wounded healer.*

12 1 Corinthians 4:5 (Good News for Modern Man).

13 Don S. Browning, *The moral context of pastoral care,* The Westminster Press, 1976.

14 William A. W. Walters & Peter Singer, *Test-tube babies,* Oxford University Press, 1982.

15 Don S. Browning, *The moral context of pastoral care,* The Westminster Press, 1976.

16 ibid.

17 Carl Wood & Ann Westmore, *Test-tube conception,* Hill of Content, 1983.

10

From Louise Brown to the Brave New World: the expanding context of IVF

Ditta Bartels

In the foregoing chapters of this book the contributors have looked at the practice and the socio-ethical issues raised by IVF largely from the perspective of infertility. We may think of this as the 'Louise Brown' context of IVF, after the first baby conceived by this technique in 1978. In this chapter we shall examine the place of IVF in a different context, namely that of biomedical research and genetic engineering.[1] To best capture this difference, we shall refer to the body of work discussed below as the 'Brave New World' context of the IVF-produced embryo.

We start by taking note of certain research developments which in due course will ensure an increasing supply of human IVF embryos. Then we enumerate the areas in which research work is likely to be carried out with these embryos. Third, we look at a range of factors which have retarded these research developments so far, but which may cease to operate in the future. Finally we propose an institutional mechanism by which the general public could participate in controlling the pace and the direction of research involving the human, IVF-generated embryo.

IVF as a source for the supply of human embryos

So far IVF has *not* generated an abundance of human embryos. Usually a woman in an IVF program is induced by means of fertility drugs to produce five or six ripe eggs or ova, and these are collected in an operation called laparoscopy. The eggs are then fertilised by her husband's sperm, so that up to five or six embryos may be available per couple. In practice, however, this number is often reduced, since not all in vitro attempts at fertilisation and subsequent embryo development are successful. In the usual IVF procedure two to three of the available embryos are inserted into the patient's uterus so as to increase the chance of an implantation. A simple calculation shows that not many developing embryos are 'left over' in such a situation.

Nevertheless a few excess embryos do result when this protocol is adhered to, and the IVF practitioners at the Queen Victoria Medical Centre in Melbourne have claimed that in part it is this excess of IVF embryos which has brought about their involvement in the embryo freezing program.[2]

Conversely, however, freezing can also be seen as leading to an *increased* availability of embryos, since in their frozen state embryos can be transported easily and gathered in appropriate collection banks. This practice has already found widespread application in the animal situation, both in the agricultural domain and in laboratory science.

In addition to freezing, there is a further technique which is likely to increase considerably the quantity of human embryos available for research purposes. This is the technique of egg ripening (or ovum maturation) in vitro. As we have seen above, in the present medical practice of IVF the patient's eggs are allowed to ripen inside the ovaries. However it is also possible to achieve egg ripening outside the body, and research is currently under way to establish the conditions for this process. Robert Edwards, the British pioneer of the IVF technique, has described his observations of externally ripening human eggs in his recent book *A matter of life*.[3]

Once in vitro egg ripening is achieved on a consistent basis, a piece of ovary tissue that is removed during a hysterectomy or other operation can provide the starting point for the production of large numbers of human embryos, since, as we all know, there are thousands of immature ova in the ovary and the procurement of human sperm is no problem. The direct relationship between the process of in vitro egg ripening and the enhanced possibilities for research on the human embryo has been recognised explicitly by the Royal Society working party on IVF:

> Recent progress in maturing eggs from rodents and other mammals in vitro raises the possibility that human ovarian tissue obtained from cadavers or removed during surgery undertaken for other purposes might

provide an alternative source of material. This would considerably enhance the scope for research on human fertilisation and embryology.[4]

In summary we can say that as the techniques of embryo freezing and in vitro egg ripening are developed, increasing numbers of human embryos will be available. Moreover, it is this availability that will occasion the shift in context of the human IVF embryo from that of infertility to that of experimentation.

Laboratory studies involving the human IVF embryo

Until now, the structure and the development of the early human embryo could hardly be investigated at all, since in the normal in vivo situation a woman does not generally know that an embryo is present until it is about 2 weeks old. By contrast, IVF-produced embryos can be examined at any stage of their development, prior to the point at which their in vitro growth terminates. According to Robert Edwards this point can be pushed out to about 9 days.

The structural and developmental study of the early human embryo is of course replete with medical relevance. It is well known that the rate of spontaneous abortion is high in humans, and that most embryos aborted spontaneously are in some way defective. The careful examination of human embryos will undoubtedly result in a better understanding of these defects, and eventually this line of inquiry will lead to treatment for infertility in cases where the problem is associated with early spontaneous abortions.

Another type of embryological investigation with great medical significance is that of using IVF-produced embryos for the study of teratogenesis, this being the faulty development of an embryo due to a harmful environment. Well-known teratogens are the German measles virus and thalidomide. By examining the effects of such teratogens on the embryo in vitro, an understanding would be gained of the corresponding processes in vivo. Indeed, the knowledge gained in such studies, coupled with the ready availability of human embryos for such work, might bring about the requirement that prior to their release onto the pharmaceutical market drugs must be tested on IVF embryos for their potentially harmful effects. It should be noted that animal embryos have limited suitability for teratogen testing since their patterns of development are quite different from the human case, and so are the environmental disturbances to their normal growth.

It has been claimed that embryonic tissue is less susceptible than adult tissue regarding the rejection mechanism which needs to be overcome when organ transplantation is carried out. For this reason, embryonic tissue derived from induced abortions has already been employed in transplantation work. In its recent report, the Australian National Health and Medical Research Council has given approval to this practice.[5] Just as embryonic organs derived from spontaneous abortions are useful for transplantation surgery, so IVF-derived embryos may also come to provide the required tissue. The American embryologist Clifford Grobstein has recently pointed out in Melbourne that in the animal case IVF embryos have been maintained in culture long enough for them to form distinct organs potentially usable for transplantation purposes.[6]

Having now considered IVF as a source of embryos for structural study, for teratogen investigations and for transplantation surgery, let us turn our attention to the ways in which IVF and genetic engineering can become joined. First we shall look at *genetic screening,* and then at *gene therapy.*

Currently the genetic screening of human foetuses is carried out by means of a procedure known as amniocentesis at about the fourteenth week of pregnancy. However animal studies indicate that genetic screening could be conducted much earlier in the pregnancy, thereby eliminating the problem of a 'long wait' for the mother. The suggested procedure consists in removing some of the cells from the early, IVF-generated embryo, and submitting these cells to chromosome or other analysis. Laboratory studies have already indicated that the IVF embryo can develop perfectly well even when some of its cells have been removed. If the genetic tests are judged to be satisfactory, the IVF embryo would be implanted in its mother. The Royal Society working group to which we have referred above has advocated that research into this IVF-based method of genetic screening be intensified.

The *sexing* of IVF-produced embryos could of course also be undertaken in this way, since the examination of chromosomes readily reveals the sex of the tested embryo. In Australia, amniocentesis-based screening, followed by the abortion of the undesired foetus, is undertaken on the basis of sex choice only in those cases where a sex-linked inherited disease is involved. However when the determination of sex is no longer preceded by an advanced pregnancy, then a parental preference for the sex of the offspring might be taken into account also in those cases where genetic disease is not the overriding consideration.

Investigating the genetic constitution of IVF-produced embryos and selectively implanting only those which are found to be normal represents an incursion of genetic engineering into the realm of IVF. A further avenue by which these two techniques can become joined is that of *inserting specific genes* into early embryos produced by IVF.

In the animal case this type of work has led to the remarkable result of the 'supermice'.[7] These are extraordinarily large mice, obtained by injecting the gene for growth hormone into mouse embryos generated by IVF. Surrogate mothers were implanted with the modified embryos, and after their birth the engineered mice grew at a much enhanced rate. In several molecular biology laboratories around the world, work is now in progress to apply the supermouse technique to livestock animals.

There is no doubt that it will still take some time before medical science is ready to correct gene defects in the early human embryo by means of an analogous procedure. However the Royal Society working group has suggested that research be fostered on gene insertion studies of *human* IVF embryos, and the U.S. President's Commission for the Study of Ethical Problems in Medicine and Biomedical Research has also emphasised the positive aspects of gene therapy at the embryo level.[8]

We should note that such a form of genetic engineering affects not only the individuals treated. The inserted genes would also be passed on to the offspring, thus extending the range of genetic modification quite considerably. The *current,* value-laden choices of biomedical practitioners and patients would thus come to exert their influence on the genetic constitution of coming generations.

Factors that so far have kept IVF in the 'Louise Brown' context

Areas of scientific investigation such as those described above undoubtedly hold enormous scientific excitement as well as considerable medical promise. But nevertheless there are indications of a moral objection from the public to this type of expansion in biomedical science and technology.[9] Indeed, there is a potential here for a conflict of interests between the ambitions of biomedical researchers to push this work ahead and to see it implemented in medical practice and, on the other hand, the resistance of the public to what is perceived as an assault on entrenched moral values.

In this section we shall look at those factors which so far have *prevented* the shift of the IVF embryo out of the 'Louise Brown' infertility context and into the 'Brave New World' context outlined briefly in the foregoing section.

Probably the major factor in keeping the IVF-generated embryo within the strict infertility context is the current difficulty in obtaining ripe eggs for in vitro fertilisation. This difficulty inevitably leads to a shortage of IVF embryos. However, as we have seen, the technique of in vitro egg ripening promises to increase the supply of IVF embryos quite considerably, and judging by the rate of progress in current biology we may be sure that this technique will be with us in the foreseeable future.

A second factor is that many of the groups currently using IVF to treat infertility have no wish to move their work out of this context. In particular, Carl Wood's group at the Queen Victoria Medical Centre in Melbourne, and the Joneses group in Virginia, U.S.A., have made it clear that their IVF work will remain within the infertility context. This is of course quite reassuring, but it is obvious that as the number of groups achieving IVF successes increases, so will the likelihood that *some* of these groups will venture forth into the 'Brave New World' domain. Not all the IVF groups will be bound by the self-imposed moral scruples of Carl Wood or the Joneses.

Third, it is possible that the local bioethics committees which have been established at most hospitals and universities would limit the production of IVF embryos to the simple infertility context. But again, while this probably applies to the Queen Victoria Medical Centre in Melbourne, where the Bioethics Committee is broadly constituted and acts in a responsible manner, the situation could well be different in many other institutions where the appropriate committees might simply rubber-stamp proposals such as the genetic engineering of IVF embryos.

Fourth, 'informed consent' could in principle operate so as to constrain the range of IVF-based work. There is no doubt, however, that *in practice* patients generally do not act as a brake with respect to the research interests of their medical practitioners.

Lastly, we should recognise that the two ends of the continuum which we have alluded to could well collapse into each other. The 'Louise Brown' infertility context can in fact be stretched so that it includes some of the 'Brave New World' context as well. Let us take the case of a couple where both partners are carriers of a genetic disease, and they have a moral objection both to a pregnancy being terminated by abortion and to artificial insemination by donor sperm. All the same, they do not wish to risk the one-in-four chance of producing a defective child. In effect they are then infertile. Now if IVF-based genetic screening or IVF-based gene therapy were available to help them, their quasi-infertility could be overcome.

Similar considerations would also apply in the other cases of embryo research examined above, e.g. the structural investigation of the IVF embryo, its employment in teratogen studies, and uses in transplantation work. The effect of this is that scientific developments which one might designate as falling within the 'Brave New World' context are brought into the purview of beneficial medical practice.

But where does this leave those who feel affronted by the use of human embryos for genetical or other biomedical research purposes? There is a need to find a way in which the future developments in this area of research can take into account not only the scientific and medical pressures driving this work ahead, but also the objections of those who feel threatened by these developments. In short, there should be an effective form of public participation for IVF-centred science and technology.

Public participation and the expanding context of IVF

So far there has not been a great deal of discussion in Australia or elsewhere on the uses of human IVF embryos for biomedical research including genetic engineering. At the moment, the Waller committee set up by the Victorian Government is about to address this issue, and a report is due in early 1984.[10] To what extent the public will be involved in decisions regarding the expansion of the IVF context remains to be seen. However, it may be argued that a report such as the one currently being prepared by the Waller committee is necessarily limited in the room that it allows for public education, discussion and decision making.

It seems to me that at the very least a *national government committee* should be established which sets up guidelines for research on the IVF embryo, monitors compliance with them, and upgrades them on a continuing basis. Furthermore, for this scrutiny process to count as a reasonable exercise in public participation, the following criteria should also be adhered to:

(1) The committee's research staff should *actively* follow the scientific progress made in the domain of animal and human embryology and genetic engineering, so that it can evaluate effectively the path and the pace of research, both in Australia and overseas.

(2) The committee's composition, deliberations and conclusions must be *publicly visible,* in particular by means of media exposure. Also, the interchange of viewpoints with the public should persist indefinitely: before drafting the guidelines, during the process of drafting, and in the ongoing phase of improving the guidelines.

(3) The guidelines must be highly specific, so that most decision making occurs at this national, publicly visible level, and does not get made piecemeal in cloistered local bioethics boards.

(4) The committee should *see* one of its main functions to lie in uncovering the *value judgments, political pressures* and *social consequences* which are involved in the science and tech- nology of embryo manipulation.

Finally, it must not be presumed that effective public participation in scientific decision making can be achieved easily. Nevertheless the effort must be made, since powerful scientific techniques such as IVF and genetic engineering can have far-reaching consequences on the health, the safety and the social attitudes of the public. It is essential that the values of those affected by science have a role to play in the determination of science's future course of development and implementation.

Statement on the author's position and status with regard to IVF

Dr Ditta Bartels is a post-doctoral research fellow in the Department of History and Philosophy of Science at the University of Wollongong, and a research affiliate in the School of Biological Sciences at the University of Sydney. She was a member of the World Council of Churches working party which prepared the document *Manipulating life: ethical issues in genetic engineering*. In the last few years Dr Bartels has written extensively on the social implications of genetic engineering and in vitro fertilisation.

1 I have elaborated these arguments in greater detail in D. Bartels, 'The uses of *in vitro* human embryos: can the public participate in decision-making?', *Search* 14, 9–10, 1983, pp. 257–62.

2 A. O. Trounson, C. Wood & J. F. Leeton, 'Freezing of embryos: an ethical obligation', *Medical Journal of Australia,* 2 October 1982, pp. 332–3.

3 R. Edwards & P. Steptoe, *A matter of life,* Hutchinson, London, 1980.

4 The Royal Society, *Human fertilisation and embryology,* Submission to DHSS Committee of Inquiry, London, 1983.

5 National Health and Medical Research Council, *Ethics in medical research involving the human fetus and human fetal tissue,* AGPS, Canberra, 1983.

6 C. Grobstein, 'In vitro fertilisation: the present climate and implications for the future', *Monash University Bioethics News* 2, 2, 1983, pp. 7–11.

7   J. G. Williams, 'Mouse and supermouse', *Nature* 300, 1982, p. 575.

8   President's Commission for the Study of Ethical Problems in Medicine and Biomedical and Behavioural Research, *Splicing life: a report on the social and ethical issues of genetic engineering with human beings,* Washington, D.C., 1982.

9   Z. Cowen, 'Questions for us all', *Medical Journal of Australia,* 2 October 1982, pp. 333–9; M. D. Kirby, 'Test-tube man', *Medical Journal of Australia,* 11 July, 1981, pp. 1–2.

10 This report is intended as a follow-up to the Waller committee's *Report on donor gametes in IVF,* Victoria, 1983. The coming report is to address three major issues: freezing and storage of embryos; surrogate mothers; use of embryos for purposes other than reproduction.

11

IVF and the wider ethical debate of genetic engineering

D. Gareth Jones

The in vitro fertilisation debate should not be viewed as an isolated phenomenon in the biomedical arena. The ethical issues raised by this debate have much in common with issues being faced in many other areas concerned with the commencement of individual human life. They take us to the heart of the relationship between much of modern biology and human society; they question the relationship between biotechnology and our perception of what it means to be human; and they bring us face to face with what, as individuals and as a society, we are prepared to sacrifice in the pursuit of an improvement in various aspects of the quality of our lives.

Neither are all the issues raised by IVF new ones. Some, such as the moral status of the embryo and the twin issues of foetal harm and foetal consent, have been debated since the early 1970s. Others, however, have emerged over the past three years or so, as the technical prospects in this area have moved rapidly into unexpected domains. Of particular interest in this context is the multifaceted challenge presented by spare embryos.

To consider IVF in the context of genetic engineering may not be strictly accurate. Nevertheless, it serves as a reminder of the potentially manipulatory powers of IVF and its associated techniques. This is not an argument against IVF *per se;* neither is it intended to distort the beneficial aspects of IVF as a means by which an infertile married couple may acquire a child of their own. But it impresses upon us the technological nature of IVF procedures, and the fact that such technology can be used in a variety of ways, some of which could prove manipulatory.

The ethical context in which IVF should be discussed, therefore, is not that of the infertile couple but of the production of children by technological means. This may seem heartless, and possibly an irrelevant approach to those caught up in the despair and tragic helplessness of a couple longing for a child. I want to argue that the approach I am proposing is the only satisfactory one in the long term. While it is true that the immediate context of the IVF debate is that of infertility, the power of the technology confronts us with questions about the nature, worthwhileness and usefulness of human embryonic material. This mixture of philosophical and pragmatic considerations cannot be evaded in the hope of short-term gains.

The technological nature of IVF is inescapable. It is a way around infertility rather than a cure for infertility. The technological expertise solves the problem in a technological manner, so that each child produced by this technique—now and in the future—will have to be produced technologically. The solution to the human dilemma of infertility is being obtained by non-human technological means. This, by itself, is not a condemnation of the technique. Nevertheless, it is a movement in the direction of increased dependence upon technology. In the long run, this may have considerable repercussions for our view of our own humanness and of human relationships.

As a tool of technology, IVF is capable of being employed in a wide variety of ways. IVF lends itself to all these applications. The alleviation of infertility is no more important than the manipulation of the embryo in ways most societies would reject. Hence, each application has to be examined on its merits. The ethical decision lies in what direction IVF should be channelled, and what priorities should be placed on its further development.

Like all technological tools, IVF is sometimes a failure. Some couples who might be expected to benefit from it fail to do so. The successes of IVF, therefore, have to be balanced against the failures, those who are disappointed and frustrated at having their last hope of a child dashed. The human face of IVF is to be seen in this balance, not in the children born to happy and grateful parents.

The element of human control in IVF has elicited two quite different responses to the procedure. The amalgam of human intervention and a laboratory environment has led some to condemn IVF as dehumanising, on the grounds that baby making and love making have been separated. Others, however, have seen the planning as being supremely human, especially since an obstacle to marital and human fulfilment has been overcome.

This is yet another aspect of the technological face of IVF. It has been argued that the laboratory production of human beings is no longer human procreation, because the technological inroads have replaced the profoundly human characteristics of normal procreation. This movement away from the physical and sexual may deprive procreation of its human connotations, since it no longer involves the diversity of factors constituting human sexual love. This could well have implications for the family as a biological unit, because the wholesale transfer of procreation to the laboratory would undoubtedly undermine the justification and support which biological parenthood gives to the monogamous marriage. These are strong arguments against the indiscriminate and widespread use of IVF. However, those children who have been conceived by IVF have been the products of marital love. What has happened is that the meaning of marital love has been transformed. The failure of the physical side of marital love has deprived it of its full human connotations. Nevertheless, it is still love, and the birth of a baby via IVF gives it a physical side it could not otherwise have had.

IVF is a dramatic extension of the sort of interference found in delivery by Caesarean section, hormonal induction of labour and artificial insemination by husband (AIH). Each of these has a legitimate place in reproductive technology, as long as there are strong therapeutic grounds for their use. Each of them can also be used unwisely. IVF should not, therefore, be regarded as a routine procedure, even when it becomes far more widespread than at present.

An argument sometimes raised against IVF is that it is an artificial means of conception, as opposed to the natural means which is regarded as the only acceptable one. The concept of the 'natural' is, however, highly relative. If it is argued that it is not natural to have a baby by IVF, it is equally unnatural to use spectacles or wear clothes made of artificial fibres. Is it unnatural to travel by car along freeways or by jumbo jet in the air? The answer must be 'yes', and yet this does not make these activities unethical.

I see no inherent objection on these grounds to IVF, where conception by natural intercourse is impossible. This is because it is important to the procreative process as a whole to assess the overall situation of the husband and wife. The potential of IVF lies in its ability to rectify a missing element in the union of husband and wife, so that it may be a legitimate means of healing in certain situations. Nevertheless, this does not justify its use as a way of bypassing the normal means of human procreation in the absence of a therapeutic rationale.

A technological form of reproduction is inferior to one involving the bodies and personalities of two individuals, and should be resorted to only when the other fails. There is no likelihood that either IVF or its technical offshoots will become a panacea for human ills, because these technological innovations are as fraught with dilemmas as are other aspects of the human predicament.

An added dimension to the ethical debate, and one implicit in the manipulatory ability of IVF, arises from procedures designed to produce spare embryos. The fertilisation of two or more eggs from a woman at any one time brings into head-on conflict pragmatic and ethical considerations. The pragmatic consideration, that the simultaneous transfer of at least two embryos increases the possibility of successful implantation, has to be balanced against the startlingly novel ethical question of our obligations regarding those embryos that are not transferred back to the woman from whom the eggs were taken.

We may contend that it is moral to carry out IVF, but that it is not moral to do anything with the resulting embryos other than reinsert them in the donor. If we adopt this position, all eggs removed from a woman and successfully fertilised will be reinserted.

On the other hand, it may be contended that spare embryos do not warrant any particular protection, since they do not possess rights, or because society has few obligations with regard to them. Under these circumstances, the spare embryos may be frozen and inserted in a later cycle into the donor, or they may be offered to another woman or to a surrogate mother, or they may be used as research tools.

Regardless of the use to which these embryos are put, the debate involves around the issue of the status of pre-implantation embryos outside the maternal body. This in turn raises issues such as whether the pre-implantation embryo is a human being, a potential human being or potential person, an entity with limited rights or an entity with no rights at all.

The possibilities are a clear indication of the conflicting values of society in this area. What is all too clear, however, is that these are far from theoretical questions. Whatever answers we give to these questions will determine what manipulations we are prepared to accept, and even encourage, on pre-implantation embryos. A Christian perspective will have to be thoroughly worked out; I favour the view that the early embryo be regarded as a potential person and therefore as an entity demanding considerable respect.

The development of current IVF technology has involved the study of pre-implantation human embryos in vitro, sometimes without any expectation that these embryos will be returned to the uterus for continued development. If the efficacy and safety of this technology are to be improved, there is a continuing need for research of this nature. A by-product of this research is that it may well contribute to a better understanding of genetic and developmental abnormalities in natural reproduction by internal fertilisation. It may also contribute to an understanding of normal and abnormal growth, teratogenesis and aspects of cancer.

This, however, is only the beginning. An inevitable extension of current studies will include the use of post-implantation stages of human development. Such studies, when feasible, would allow analyses of many aspects of organ, tissue and cell maturation, and would allow the culture of individual types of embryonic tissue—such as nervous tissue. Such tissues would prove of immense value in helping unravel the intricacies of tissue and cell differentiation. These, in turn, may have important clinical applications, dependent on the use of cultured foetal organs and tissues as replacements for defective organs and tissues in children and adults.

The question we have to face is whether this is the direction in which we wish to go. It is quite a new direction because it entails the use of human material. While there will be differences of opinion on precisely what is the best way of describing human embryonic tissue, most would accept that a human embryo is different from a rat embryo or a mouse embryo. For most people, including myself, human life is different from non-human life, and this has ethical implications from which we cannot escape.

Guidelines regarding the use of human embryos in research have been drawn up by a number of organisations in both Australia and the United Kingdom since late 1982. They all raise a plethora of contentious issues and bring into the open the intense conflict between the demands for greater knowledge and respect for human embryos. When the two are pitted against each other, something has to give. There is no problem for those who believe that the embryo has no rights. There are immense problems for everyone else, no matter at what stage of embryonic development they decide the embryo should be allowed rights and dignity.

This is illustrated by an editorial in the British journal *Nature* (28 April 1983) when commenting on the guidelines issued by the Royal Society. These, according to the editorial, are based 'on the proposition that an early embryo is not a living thing, in the sense of being potentially autonomously self-replicating, but rather a kind of passing parasite, dependent on a uterus for full development'. For those with this perspective there is no problem, except to decide at what stage during embryonic development this state of affairs changes. And this is an issue which has received virtually no attention up to the present time.

The question remains: what is the moral and biological status of the early human embryo? Can an answer be based solely on scientific criteria (if such criteria exist) or must it have reference to specific ethical and moral viewpoints? The desire to find a strictly scientific answer is a strong one, especially for those with no religious position. It has been suggested by Clifford Grobstein that the pre-implantation embryo does not function as a multicellular organism. Consequently the pre-implantation period can be regarded as a period of pre-individuality.

Such viewpoints, however, ignore the *potential* of human embryos, namely that they have the potential to become human beings in the fullest sense. To isolate any embryo from this future dimension, and to treat it as though it was an end in itself *as an embryo,* is to fragment the history of an individual human being.

This is not to suggest that human embryos must be treated as if they were fully developed human beings. What it does stress is that they should not be treated simply as a *means to an end,* that end being the pursuit of scientific and medical information.

Ethical issues concerning laboratory IVF bring into focus one's view of the early embryo. If it is not regarded as human, laboratory IVF research may pose few problems since concern about damage to the embryo and about the fate of the embryo do not arise. On the other hand, once the potentially human characteristics of the embryo are taken into account, research of this type raises profound ethical considerations. This is because experiments on living embryos can only be carried out by denying their possible viability and their potential significance as human beings. Once this is done, however innocently by most researchers, the way has been opened to all the possible applications of IVF. It is at this point that we are confronted in stark terms with the manipulatory side of IVF. The fundamental issue, from which there can be no escape, is whether respect should be shown to human embryos in view of their potential for full humanness, or whether they should be treated as non-human experimental material.

This is the basic ethical choice underlying research on human embryos. Once they are regarded as nothing more than dispensable experimental material, no logically consistent limits can be placed on the whole range of feasible IVF applications. Although most of those involved in current IVF infertility research may not wish to go beyond the bounds of infertility, only ethically determined limits will prevent this happening. And these limits, whatever they may be, will stem from an assessment of the value of embryonic and foetal material. In practical terms, we are faced with the challenge of whether research on human embryonic material should continue. If in the light of the potential of this material for full humanness we decide that such research should not continue, there will be repercussions. Any limitation on laboratory IVF research will inhibit the expansion of our knowledge of reproductive embryonic development. In my opinion this is a sacrifice we shall have to make if we are to retain control over human experimentation.

A closely related consideration is that the way in which information is obtained is itself of importance. It may even be that this is of greater importance than the resulting information. Hence, if information is obtained unethically, the chances that it will be applied unethically are very high. Of course, it has first to be determined whether experimentation on living human embryos is unethical. But, if it is, that is of profound significance for the way in which the resulting data are used and for the way in which yet further information is obtained. If human embryos, no matter how early in development they may be, are produced with the express purpose of simply providing scientific information, that information has already taken precedence over the significance of human existence. It should be obvious, therefore, that one of the most difficult ethical issues in IVF as currently employed emanates from the freezing of spare embryos. Once embryos are frozen, a decision regarding their future will have to be taken at some stage. By far the simplest course of action from an ethical angle is to desist from using hormone stimulation of the woman's ovaries. There are then no spare embryos and hence no frozen embryos. The choice in this instance is between clinical efficiency and ethical acceptability.

Once clinical efficiency is the course of choice, spare embryos will be available as research material or they may be discarded. In practice, however, once the pragmatic course of producing spare embryos has been embarked upon, the most likely next step will also be a pragmatic one, namely the use of the spare material as a source of scientific information. To discard this material would, in the eyes of those involved in such programs, be a waste of valuable material.

I find it difficult to resist this argument, even though it can also be argued that the death of spare embryos is the most ethical course of action. It is most akin to what would happen naturally. However, human intervention has been so prominent in the production and maintenance of spare embryos that to allow them to 'die' is out of character with all that has gone on before.

Once spare embryos are produced, and as long as they are superfluous to the therapeutic needs of the donor, they will probably be used for research. Nevertheless, I have grave doubts about experimentation on living human embryos even when the embryos are over and above those required in a clinical IVF program. To class such embryos as 'pre-embryos' does not get around the problem of their potential for humanness. While it is true that early human embryos do not possess internal conscious awareness, they do possess the potential for this awareness. However understandable the reasons behind the legitimisation of this research, the borderline between this research and laboratory IVF is a very fine one. The only sure way around this dilemma is to refrain from producing spare embryos.

Underlying much debate over these matters is the assumption that the moral status of the embryo changes at the point of implantation. This is quite unsubstantiated, and appears to be principally based on the subjective feeling that something which is small and very immature has less worth than something which is larger and more mature.

There is an ambivalence about IVF from which we cannot escape. One would like to give a simple answer on the legitimacy, or otherwise, of IVF. But this is not possible.

IVF and embryo transfer, as a means of treating infertility, are compatible with a respect for embryonic and potential human life. The death of spare embryos parallels the death of numerous embryos during normal internal fertilisation. Since embryonic wastage is the price that has to be paid for the birth of a normally conceived child, it is hardly surprising that it also has to be paid in IVF.

Risks are taken in nature; so must they be in the laboratory. If the risks of the laboratory procedure are no greater than those usually found, they do not constitute grounds against IVF. After all, harm to foetuses and children does not only come from IVF. It comes from pregnant women smoking cigarettes and drinking alcohol, from a lack of parental affection for a child, from poor nutrition before and after birth, and from family break-up. IVF, therefore, must be viewed in the broad context of human relationships and aspirations.

The possible applications of IVF, however, far outrun that of infertility, and extend well beyond the alleviation of infertility in married couples. From my own Christian perspective, IVF should be limited to married couples because only in this way will it enhance human relationships rather than diminish them. It should be used to support family ties and strengthen natural biological roots within a family.

IVF is legitimate if it helps a married couple have a child of their own; a child derived from their own bodies, an outcome of their marriage. In this way, it serves a therapeutic purpose. This is an acceptable goal, but it must be seen within the context of family love and the marital bond. If it is used to allow everyone to have a child regardless of family ties and obligations, it becomes a threat to family life. For those with a high view of family life, ovum transfer into the uterus of a woman from whom it did not come, the fertilisation of eggs and sperm from other than married couples, surrogate motherhood, cloning and human−animal hybrids are not acceptable.

It is not a question of whether IVF is wholly good or wholly evil. Some aspects of IVF programs have far-reaching ethical implications and IVF itself has consequences for societies' attitudes towards issues such as abortion and adoption. The agony of infertility dare not be ignored; but neither dare we ignore the multitude of ramifications which the manipulation of embryos may have for our view of the significance of the whole human endeavour. It is for this reason that, in the final analysis, IVF needs to be viewed in the very much broader context of biomedical technology and genetic engineering.

Annotated bibliography

A selection of bioethical readings with a particular focus on in vitro fertilisation

Trevor Hogan

ANGLICAN CHURCH OF AUSTRALIA (GENERAL SYNOD) SOCIAL RESPONSIBILITIES COMMISSION. *Issues File* (January 1984).
Includes all official statements made by the Commission on bioethical issues over the past two years. Available from the Rev. A. Nichols, Secretary, Social Responsibilities Commission, c/- 8 Batman Street, West Melbourne, Vic. 3003.

ASCHE, THE HON. MR JUSTICE. AID, IVF and genetic engineering— beyond the legal frontiers. Address given to the College of Law and Family Law Practitioners Association of New South Wales. The David Opas Memorial Lecture, 43 pp., unpublished, 30 July 1983.

BEAUCHAMP, TOM L. & CHILDRESS, JAMES F. *Principles of biomedical ethics.* Oxford University Press, N.Y., 1979.

BRITISH COUNCIL OF CHURCHES AND FREE CHURCH FEDERAL COUNCIL. *Choices in childlessness.* By a Working Group under the direction of the Very Rev. Peter Baeltz, Dean of Durham, March 1982.

CHURCH OF ENGLAND (GENERAL SYNOD) BOARD FOR SOCIAL RESPONSIBILITY. *Evidence to the DHSS (Warnock) inquiry into human fertilisation and embryology.* 14 pp. CIO Publishing, London, March 1983.

CHURCH OF ENGLAND. The Mothers Union (Social Concern Committee). Statement to the government inquiry into human fertilisation and embryology. 6 pp. London, February 1983.

CONOLLY, THOMAS J. (ed.). *Health care in crisis: a bioethical perspective.* Laurdel Bioethics Foundation, Sydney, 1982.
Essentially a compilation of papers presented and reports of panel discussions during a conference held at the University of N.S.W., August 1981. This book of readings provides a comprehensive smorgasbord of views, values and issues in the bioethical field of health care. Contributors include Mr Justice Lusher, D. Overduin, P. Singer, R. Scott and H. Kuhse.

EDWARDS, ROBERT & STEPTOE, PATRICK. *A matter of life: the story of a medical breakthrough.* Hutchinson & Co., London, 1980.

The Hastings Center Report: Annual Bibliography of Bioethics.
Includes sections on general philosophical ethics and theological ethics as well as sections by issue (e.g. IVF).

JOHNSTONE, BRIAN. 'In vitro fertilisation: some moral questions'. *National Outlook,* June 1981.

McCORMICK, RICHARD A., SJ. *How brave a new world? dilemmas in bioethics.* SCM Press, London, 1981.

MONASH UNIVERSITY CENTRE FOR BIOETHICS. *Bioethics News,* vol. 1, 1983.
A quarterly edited by Helga Kuhse containing occasional papers and news of recent developments in biomedical ethics.

MONASH UNIVERSITY CENTRE FOR HUMAN BIOETHICS. *Ethical implications in the use of donor sperm, eggs and embryos in the treatment of human infertility.* Proceedings of the conference held on 4 May 1983. Ed. Frank D. Giantomasso, Melbourne, 1983.
A useful booklet of readings containing papers delivered at the seminar and including four main sections:
1. Scientific perspectives
2. Religious perspectives
3. Social and psychological aspects
4. Legal aspects
Particularly noteworthy contributions were made by Fr John Boyd-Boland (who proffers a 'liberal' Catholic perspective), Ms Eva Learner and Ms Jennifer Hunt.

NATIONAL HEALTH AND MEDICAL RESEARCH COUNCIL. *Ethics in medical research.* Adopted by the Council at its 94th Session, October 1982. AGPS, Canberra, 1983.

Incorporates notes on:
- institutional ethics committees
- research on children, the mentally ill and those in dependent relationships or comparable situations
- therapeutic trials
- in vitro fertilisation and embryo transfer

NATIONAL HEALTH AND MEDICAL RESEARCH COUNCIL. *Ethics in medical research involving the human fetus and human fetal tissue.* Adopted by the Council at its 96th Session, October 1983. AGPS, Canberra. 1983.

OVERDUIN, DANIEL CH. & FLEMING, JOHN I. *Life in a test-tube: medical and ethical issues facing society today.* Lutheran Publishing House, Adelaide, 1982.

John Fleming, a contributor to this volume and a member of the Social Responsibilities Commission, teams up with Lutheran theologian Dr Daniel Overduin to provide a critical examination of the development of medical research.

REICH, WARREN T. (editor in chief). *Encyclopedia of bioethics.* 4 vols. The Free Press, a division of Macmillan Publishers, N.Y., 1978.

ST VINCENT'S BIOETHICS CENTRE. *Newsletter,* vol. 1, 1983.

A quarterly newsletter reviewing scientific developments from a Roman Catholic perspective.

SANTAMARIA, J. G. & TONTI-FILIPINI, N. (eds). *Science and ethics in the treatment of infertility: the search for a Catholic response.*

'This book, soon to be published by the St Vincent's Bioethics Centre, is a collection of articles by lawyers, theologians, philosophers and medical practitioners, including two gynaecologists, a micro-surgeon, an endocrinologist and a psychiatrist. It is an attempt to provide a layman's guide to the medical problems of infertility, its causes, diagnosis, prognosis, and the various treatments currently available. The ethical, theological and legal problems are dealt with in separate chapters and the concluding chapter provides an analysis of the search for ethical and legal guidelines . . . this book sets out to examine the issues involved in the medical treatment of infertility in the light of the traditional Catholic understanding of human nature.'

U.S. PRESIDENT'S COMMISSION FOR THE STUDY OF ETHICAL PROBLEMS IN MEDICINE AND BIOMEDICAL AND BEHAVIOURAL RESEARCH. *Splicing life: a report on the social and ethical issues of genetic engineering with human beings.* Washington, D.C., 1982.

VARGA, ANDREW C. *The main issues in bioethics.* Paulist Press, Ramsey, N.J., 1980.

VICTORIA. COMMITTEE TO CONSIDER THE SOCIAL, ETHICAL AND LEGAL ISSUES ARISING FROM IN VITRO FERTILISATION. *Report on donor gametes in IVF.* 68 pp. August 1983.
   Includes the Issues Paper on *Donor gametes in IVF,* 32 pp., April 1983. Available from the Victorian Law Reform Commission.

WALTERS, LEROY (ed.). *Bibliography of bioethics,* vols 1–8. Center for Bioethics, Kennedy Institute of Ethics, Georgetown University, Washington, D.C. The Free Press, Macmillan, New York.
   A comprehensive bibliography; it covers all bioethical issues and provides a concise listing of all relevant readings (annual publication).

WALTERS, LEROY. 'Human in vitro fertilisation: a review of the ethical literature'. *The Hastings Center Report,* August 1979, pp. 23–43.
   This essay is a comprehensive overview of the ethical literature available in published form until December 1978. We refer readers to this paper for references prior to 1979. Note also that Leroy Walters conducts a survey of bioethical literature for *The Hastings Center Report* each year in addition to the above two listed sources.

WALTERS, PROFESSOR WILLIAM & SINGER, PROFESSOR PETER (eds). *Test-tube babies: a guide to moral questions, present techniques and future possibilities.* Oxford University Press, Melbourne, 1982.
   Probably the most well-known book of readings and the first of its kind in Australia on the subject matter of IVF. Contributors include A. Rassaby, H. Kuhse, W. Walters, P. Singer, J. Morgan and W. Daniel. For a more analytical review of this book see Dr Brian Scarlett's review, 'When is a human in being?', in *Australian Book Review,* no. 44, September 1982, p. 32.

WILLIAMS, P. & STEVENS, G. 'What now for test tube babies?'. *New Scientist,* 4 February 1982, pp. 312–16.

WOOD, PROFESSOR CARL & WESTMORE, ANN. *Test-tube conception: a guide for couples, doctors and the community to the revolutionary breakthrough in treating infertility including the ethical, legal and social issues.* Hill of Content, Melbourne, 1983.
   A useful and easy to read introduction to medical developments in the field, along with a discussion on the problems of infertility. As a guide to the 'ethical, legal and social issues', however, it is inadequate. It would have been more honest of the authors if they had

used the heading for chapter 9 as the subtitle of the whole book, i.e. 'Justification of the procedure'.

WORLD COUNCIL OF CHURCHES. *Faith and science in an unjust world.* Report of the WCC Conference on Faith, Science and the Future. WCC, Geneva, 1980.
   Vol. 1: Plenary Representations (Section 4)
   Vol. 2: Reports and Recommendations (Part One; Chapter V)

WORLD COUNCIL OF CHURCHES. *Manipulating life: ethical issues in genetic engineering.* Church and Society, WCC, Geneva, 1983.

YOUNG, ROBERT. The ethics of in vitro fertilisation. Paper read at ANZAAS, Macquarie University, 11 May 1982, as part of a session on Perspectives of in vitro fertilisation.

Glossary of terms
commonly used in artificial reproductive technology

Abortion Spontaneous or induced termination of pregnancy before embryo or foetus is capable of sustaining life on its own.

Amniocentesis Technique of withdrawing fluid around foetus prior to birth to enable diagnosis of abnormalities.

Artificial insemination Injection of semen into the vagina by artificial means. AID is when semen is provided by donor, AIH by husband.

Blastocyst Early embryo stage having form of a single layer of cells around a fluid-filled cavity about five days after fertilisation.

Chromosome Nucleic acid containing hereditary factors.

Clone A colony of cells identical with and arising from a single parent.

Cryopreservation A freezing process allowing embryos to be preserved indefinitely in a state of suspended animation.

Cyst Sac-like structure containing fluid.

De-oxy-ribonucleic acid (DNA) Hereditary protein material of the cell found in the chromosomes of the cell nucleus.

Down's syndrome Chromosomal disorder resulting in mental retardation and physical defects; also known as mongolism.

Ectogenesis Growth of foetus outside the human body without need for human womb.

Egg Female cell from ovary which results in an embryo when fused with a male sperm cell.

Embryo In humans, developing fertilised egg until eighth week of pregnancy.

Embryo transfer   Transfer of early embryo, after fertilisation of egg in vitro in the laboratory, to the womb.

Eugenics   Study of possible influences as a means of improving the hereditary characteristics of a race.

Fallopian tube   Tube along which an egg travels from ovary to uterus, and in which the egg is fertilised.

Fertilisation   Fusion of an egg and sperm cell.

Foetus   Embryo from the end of the eighth week of pregnancy until birth.

Gamete   Cell concerned with reproduction—e.g. the egg and sperm cells.

Genetic engineering   Manipulation of genes by scientific means in a laboratory.

Idiopathic infertility   Infertility of unknown cause.

Implantation   Attachment of embryo to lining of the uterus, occurring six or seven days after fertilisation of the egg.

In vitro   'In glass'; e.g. in a test tube.

In vivo   In the life situation.

Laparoscopy   Procedure to enable visual inspection of internal organs and collection of human eggs from the ovaries.

Recombinant DNA technology   Splicing of genes of two unrelated organisms and their insertion into a host organism.

Surrogate mother   Substitute mother who bears a child for a woman who cannot bear children herself.

Zygote   Early stage of the embryo after fertilisation.

Index

Numbers refer to pages; *g* to glossary definitions; *n* to notes.